Garage Sale of the Mind and Other Opinions

To one of our best and brightest.

I look forward to your first book.

Jim Hill

Garage Sale of the Mind and Other Opinions

Jim Hills

Garage Sale of the Mind and Other Opinions

Copyright © 2015 Jim Hills.
All rights reserved.

Most of the essays and articles in this book have appeared in a variety of periodicals over the past twenty-five years.

You can write to the author at jhills@corban.edu.

Additional copies of this book are available for sale online at
www.CreateSpace.com
www.BooksaMillion.com
www.BarnesandNoble.com
www.Amazon.com

In memory of
James Anderson, Scott Becker,
Nancy Beers and Sue Seiber,
my students and friends,
and of our conversations
too soon interrupted.

Contents

I.   **Friends and Family**, 11

    Thanksgiving Table, 13

    Love When We Need Love Most, 19

    Achieving Excellence, 23

    The Tyler Principle, 31

    Endure Hardness as a Good Soldier, 37

    Saying It Our Way, 45

    Out of the Ivory Palaces, 53

    Homecoming, 59

    Big Mike, 65

    Tony Giacoletti, 71

    Beside the Still Waters, 77

    Having the Time of Your Life, 83

    Acquainted with Grief, 89

    At the Funeral of James Anderson, 95

    On Eagles' Wings, 99

II.   **The Seven Deadly Sins**, 105

    The Seven Deadly Sins, 107

    Greed, 109

Gluttony, 115

Wrath, 121

Lust, 127

Sloth, 133

Envy, 139

Pride, 145

III. The Classic Christian Virtues, 151

Patience, 153

Self-Control, 159

Love, 165

Gratitude, 171

Compassion, 177

Faith, 183

Humility, 189

IV. Remembering 9/11, 195

A Moment of Silence, 197

Ground Zero: A Test of the Heart, 203

V. Church, Politics and Society, 209

Christianity as Commodity, 211

Garage Sale of the Mind, 217

Courtesy, 223

Apples of Gold in Settings of Silver, 229

Dressing for Christian Success, 237
A Welcome for the Heroes, 245
The Courage of Everlasting Life, 251
The New View, 259
Reasonable Service, 267
The Catalogue of Kitsch, 273
Radical Subjectivity, 279
Biblical Economics, 289
Wearing the Yellow Jersey, 295

VI. Sometimes You Just Gotta Laugh, 301
The Next Step, 303
Sometimes You Just Gotta Laugh, 307
Eating In, 315

VII. Bible Stories, 325
No Scorekeeping, 327
Speech Seasoned with Salt, 333
A Better Way, 339
People of Hope, 345
The Road, 351
The Invitation, 355
Two Sparrows, 361
Great Expectations, 367
Don't Be Anxious, 373

Undoing the Damage, 379

Power Restored, 387

Reviewing, 391

VIII. Conversations with My Students, 397

The Principle of Nearest at Hand, 399

Consider This..., 405

A Brave Heart for the Future, 407

Telling the Truth about Writing, 411

A Word to the Rookies, 417

The Loud, Long Cataract of Sound, 421

Commencement 2013, 427

Exit Exam, 431

About the Author, 435

Friends and Family

Thanksgiving Table

December 2009

At the Thanksgiving table I find myself ill at ease. At first glance everything seems familiar. Most of the clan is here: Dad, Mom, and Grandma, in good appetite for all of her ninety-six years; my two brothers and their sons, Brian and Mark; Jodi, my niece, and her husband, Charlie; my wife and I and our two boys; Kevin, my daughter's boyfriend; and Cathy herself, in her second year at the Atkinson Graduate School of Management here in Salem, Oregon.

The talk is familiar too, most of it. This is a family of athletes, and for an hour or so before dinner the men have kept an eye on the Detroit-Minnesota game, rehearsed favorite sports stories, and offered predictions on the NFL playoff possibilities and the upcoming basketball season.

There are stories of the annual Alaska salmon expedition. Summers, my brother Tim guides on the Gulkana River. Brian goes with him, and so do my sons. There my older son, Andrew, taught his younger brother how to tie a proper knot, how to cast, and how to hook and land fifty-pound king salmon.

The fishermen all have stories of big fights—powerful fish leaping and running, peeling off line so fast that if you put your thumb down on your screaming reel, you'll be blistered in an instant—stories of the ones that got away, and the ones that didn't, and reports of bald eagles along the bank, of moose and caribou sightings.

Many of the stories have been told before, but no matter. Telling and hearing them again is a way of enjoying it all once more, of enjoying one another, and of giving thanks.

In the kitchen, too, things proceed as usual. Jo Anne, Tim's wife, has brought her championship rolls and a counter full of pies. Mom has remembered my fondness for green olives, and has supplied a full bowl of them, green and tart. "Go on, now," the women say when we men stroll into the kitchen, stooping to sniff the rolls or trying to lift a toasted nut from the pecan pie. "There are vegetables and dip in the living room. You won't starve. We'll let you know when everything's ready. Go watch your game."

It's a good-natured and familiar scold, but the women seem to mean it. They have their stories too, and information on recipes and impending births and how the kids are doing in school. And how life is changing as, one by one, the children grow to adulthood and leave home.

Our gathering this year is at Cathy's house, and this is what I find unsettling. She's twenty-three now, and feels strongly that it's time for her to have her own place.

Cathy has always been independent. She could have commuted to college, but chose to live at school, not so much to avoid the forty-mile drive as to begin to stake out her own life, away from the parental roof. I missed her, but I approved of her decision. Her first year of graduate school, to save money, she lived at home, though she was seldom here, spending long hours in class, at the library, and at work. Last summer her job often required her to catch an early Monday flight to California or New York.

But all this time her address, her real address, was my address. When she finished the school term or ended her European stay or finished her work week, she came home, and home was her father's house.

Now it's different. She and two of her school friends have rented a house, three miles from my place. The roommates made Thanksgiving plans for elsewhere, and Cathy asked her mother and her aunt if the festivities could be held at her new place.

It could, and here we are.

"Dad, you sit there," Cathy instructs me now. She glows with the heat of the kitchen, and with proprietary pride. She's given me a tour of the house. "I love this place," she said. I could see that. And I could see how wide her orbit was swinging, how far it was likely to go. "I'm thinking of looking for a job in Seattle," she told me. "I love it up there, and I hear the job market is pretty good."

Well, this is what we've been working toward all along, I remind myself. *From teaching her how to hold a spoon, to how to drive a stick shift; from watching her first steps, to watching her walk across the platform to get her diploma, you've been aiming toward this. Enjoy remembering what she was, and be thankful for what she is.*

These smart, beautiful young women, these strong, swift young men—"our children," we say. But we have never owned them. They've been entrusted to us by a heavenly Father wiser and more loving than we. They are His. And now, if we want them with us, we have to let them go.

Around seven o'clock the exodus begins. My parents leave, then Jodi and Charlie, and my brothers and their families. The rented tables are folded and laid against the living room wall. "I'll come back in the morning and run those back to the rental place," I say to Cathy.

"No need," she says. "Kevin will come by and we'll take them back in his Blazer."

"Sure," Kevin says. "No trouble at all."

Ten days later I'm getting ready to teach my 11:00 class when my office phone rings. "Dad?" a cheerful voice says. "It's Cathy."

"Hi, Babe. What can I do for you?"

"Nothing. I just called to thank you for looking at that marketing report for me."

"Sure," I say. "No problem."

"And—thanks for the check. It really helped me out."

"You're welcome."

"I'll pay you back someday."

"I know you will."

"Well, that's all I called for," she says. "I've gotta go."

"Yes," I say. "Thanks for the call." I grab my book and my notes and shut the door behind me.

Halfway down the hall, I realize I am whistling.

Love When We Need Love Most

May 1996

It happens without fail when a mother brings her newborn to church. After the morning service my wife calls me over. "Look at him," she says, smiling that smile of women in the presence of infants. "Isn't he beautiful? He looks just like Charlie, don't you think?"

The young mother lifts her gaze from the baby in her arms to me. I do not like these moments. The truth is, I do not find this baby especially beautiful, and no, I don't see that he looks much like his father, who, in any case, is not beautiful either.

"Umm, cute baby," I say. "Has his dad's, uh, ears. Listen, David says he's hungry. We're ready to go when you are."

David is hungry much of the time. He's sixteen. On a Tuesday evening I sit in the bleachers and watch him play softball. He's an outfielder on a men's city-league team. My older son, Andy, age twenty-four, plays first base. David looks frail out there, surrounded by two-hundred-pound men twice his age.

What happens to all the food he eats?

But he's hardly frail. He rips the first pitch of the game into left for a single. When the next batter singles to short right David is a brief study in grace and speed, leaning in against centrifugal force as he flashes around second and swoops into third. The right fielder makes a quick appraisal of David's speed and flips the ball to the second baseman. "Beautiful," I say. "Ooo, that boy can run. Looks like his dad."

He gets two more hits in that game, the first of a double-header. In the second game he collects two more hits, and with two out in the seventh inning Andy homers to tie the game. I'm enjoying this.

My wife has mixed feelings about our sons' stations in life, Andy grown and David, the youngest of our four children, soon to begin his junior year of high school. And the girls: Heather, the oldest, has two children of her own, and Cathy, one year of M.B.A. work behind her, has a summer job that takes her in and out of airports all over the country.

"My babies are all grown," Bonnie says. "How did it happen so fast?"

I think about this as I watch my sons tattoo the ball. I remember the round-the-clock feedings, the teething, the ear infections, the changing and the bathing. I like this better. After the game Dave will be hungry. We'll get something to eat, review the game, discuss who the Trail Blazers might get in the NBA draft. Better, in my view, than powdering his infant backside or trying to spoon mushed carrots between his little gums.

Mothers are amazing people. They seem to be at their best when we're least attractive and most helpless. They do the dirty work without much comment. "I never thought about laundry before," one of my freshman students told me. "It was just there, clean and folded. I had no idea my mom spent so much time doing that for me."

Sunday afternoon Dave and I sit together watching the NBA draft. Commissioner David Stern steps to the lectern, opens an envelope and announces that the Golden State Warriors, picking first, choose Joe Smith, of the University of Maryland.

Joe Smith, all six feet nine and a half inches of him, grins, pulls a Warriors cap onto his large head, and strides off to be interviewed. In the audience his mother, tears streaming down her cheeks, stands and raises her hands. It's easy to read her lips. "Thank You," she says. "Thank You. Thank You, Jesus."

How many meals have vanished into Joe Smith's

powerful body? How many hours at the stove for Mrs. Smith? How many loads of laundry? How many rides to the gym? How many prayers?

I speak now for all sons and husbands. Thank You. Thank You, God, for these good women, mothers and wives who see us at our best and our worst, and who love us when we need it most.

Achieving Excellence

June 1982

The small girl on the top step of the winner's platform grinned as the medals, dangling from red, white, and blue ribbons, accumulated around her neck. Balance beam: gold; uneven parallel bars: silver; vault: gold; floor exercise: gold; all-around: gold. She had been the top point winner in every dual meet this season, Saturday after Saturday, and now she was leaving the Oregon Class IV State Championships, in which dozens of girls competed, with four golds and a silver.

On this day she had made it all look easy, the pirouettes and split leaps on a four-inch-wide beam; the spins, drops, and catches from one bar to another; the launching of a tightly compressed body off a springboard to a quick handspring off the leather horse to a precisely controlled landing on the mat; the flashing, twisting leaps and aerial somersaults of the floor routine, every motion synchronized to music, and all done with a bright smile that suggested this was all great fun, no trouble at all. It was only as spectators watched so many others misstep, stumble or fall that the difficulty of these moves became apparent.

Excellence is like that. Accomplished athletes, poets, and singers make the excruciatingly difficult seem effortless. But behind the perfectly thrown pass, the flawless sonnet, and the soaring aria lies a rich history of talent, training, and experience.

I knew the story behind those medals decorating my daughter's neck. It began with a gift—a small, muscular body with an unusually high strength-to-weight ratio and startling quickness. My wife one day spied Cathy, age four, clamping her fingers and bare toes to the thin edges of a door jamb and climbing like a monkey up to the lintel, where she hung from the tips of her small fingers, swinging cheerfully.

Not long afterward we took her to a gym. "Well," the coach said, "she's younger than the rest of my students, but okay, I'll take her on."

Within a couple of months he told us, "This girl has a gift. I think she can become a very good gymnast."

She did. But her natural talent was only the first step on the way to the winner's stand. The daily conditioning alone was enough to crush the less determined: forty pull-ups, fifty push-ups, two hundred sit-ups, painful stretches to gain flexibility, sprint after sprint up flights of stairs. And this was just the beginning of a practice session. Each move on the floor or the apparatus was made again and again, created and refined to the smallest detail. "More extension!" the coach ordered. "Point the toes! Carry your arms higher!"

Missteps on the beam produced bone-deep bruises. An hour on the bars sometimes tore calluses off her hands, leaving them raw and bloody. There were rib-rattling falls so frightening that I stopped watching her workouts. One night an especially difficult practice session left her so exhausted her trembling legs could barely carry her to the car.

She read the question on my face. "It's all right, Dad," she said. "It's worth it. This is what you have to do to be the best. I like winning."

But not even her talent and training had meant instant victories. She had worked hard to get ready for her first meet, only to finish far back in the pack. "I didn't do very well today," she muttered afterward. "I'm better than that. What happened?"

"Well," I said, "your coach says you were the youngest gymnast out there. You're just a rookie. You need experience. Keep at it; you're going to do well."

And, of course, she did, rising to a level of excellence that brought her a wall full of ribbons and medals. The secret? There was no secret, only a very old, tested recipe: talent, training, and experience. And in spite of the dozens of expensive seminars and shelves of books on the subject of excellence it's doubtful that much needs to be said beyond that trio of simple words whose value is supported by history and Scripture.

In 1 Corinthians chapter twelve Paul listed some of the gifts that God has given to His people. Two inferences can be drawn from a reading of this passage: the list is not exhaustive, and we are to have a clear idea of how we can best serve. That is, we ought to take an accurate inventory of ourselves to recognize what we can do best and what we may best leave to others.

To return to an athletic metaphor, if we're short, slow, and clumsy we ought to understand that no amount of training will turn us into a top-flight basketball player. And most of us have no hope of ever hitting a major league curve ball, no matter how many hours we might spend in the batting cage. Excellence begins with talent, a gift from God.

We have all been given something: a way with children, a pleasant voice, a flair for language, a knack for mechanics, an eye for color and design, adroitness with needle and thread, a quick and agile mind. We remember Barnabas' business acumen, Daniel's administrative skills, Dorcas' tailoring ability, and Paul's powerful intellect.

Clearly, each of these people had a special ability. But their accomplishments didn't just come about because they were talented. They trained hard. We know something about the preparation of Daniel and Paul, for example. Before God used them in unusual ways, they studied for years, developing and refining their mental powers.

Daniel was one of the captive Jews sent to Babylon for Chaldean training because he was already "skillful in all wisdom, and cunning in knowledge, and understanding science," with the ability to "stand in the king's palace." In Babylon he undertook an intensive three-year program of training and study. Only after this was he prepared to hold the influential post in the Babylonian government that made possible his brilliant career.

Paul's preparation was equally lengthy and strenuous. He studied under Gamaliel, one of the leading rabbis of the century, and his seat on the Sanhedrin indicated that other Jewish scholars and leaders considered Paul—then Saul—worthy of honor and trust.

After his experience on the road to Damascus, he told the church at Galatia, he "went into Arabia," apparently to think through his radical conversion, and then returned to Damascus.

After three years he went to Jerusalem to visit with Peter. Altogether, some thirteen or fourteen years of study and work marked the time from Paul's conversion to his first missionary journey, and at least another year of faithful labor passed before he wrote the first of his Biblical epistles.

Finally, excellence is built on experience. A bishop, or overseer, Paul told Timothy, must not be a novice. And deacons, he said, must be "proved." Biblical leadership, and the life of excellence that it implies, is founded not on some secret of success or even on talent alone, but on years of informed service and experience.

Experience is knowledge applied in action. It may be the only way to acquire the kind of sound judgment which seldom encounters the unforeseen. In a culture that overvalues youth and image, it is well to remind ourselves that the leaders of the first century church were called "elders," a title indicative of experience and substance.

Above all, for the Christian, the pursuit of excellence is an exercise not in ego, but in humility. Our talents are a gift from God, as are the strength and years to develop and employ those talents.

Some say that excellence, like virtue, is its own reward. But for the Christian there's something more: the promise of the Author of excellence, of Excellence Himself, saying, "Well done, thou good and faithful servant...enter thou into the joy of thy Lord."

The Tyler Principle

July 1993

One summer day my grandson, not quite three, noticed that he and I are not the same color. We had been to town together, and as he sat beside me in the car on the way home he peered at my right hand on the steering wheel. The knuckle on my little finger was slightly inflamed.

"Grandpa," he said. "Why is your hand pink?"

"Well, Ty, it looks as though I bumped or scratched that knuckle, and I have fair skin. That's just the color it gets."

He stretched out his own small arm and examined it. "Well," he said finally, "I'm brown."

"That's right," I said, and waited for the next question.

"Grandpa?"

"Yes, Ty?"

"Can we go to Taco Bell?"

In his mind there were no inferences to be drawn from the fact that he and I have different levels of melanin. There were more important issues. He was hungry, he knew what he wanted for lunch, and his grandfather, experience had taught him, was a likely source of cash. The difference in our skin tone was duly noted, then apparently filed under "mildly interesting but not significant."

There was a sweet wisdom in this. What mattered, what had always mattered, was that we are members of the same family. I am grandfather. Not blue-eyed grandfather, straight-haired grandfather, light-skinned grandfather. Grandfather, plain and simple.

I call it the Tyler Principle: family trumps color. It's a simple idea, but apparently not universally obvious.

Some questions are understandable. "Did you adopt him?" a stranger in the grocery store asked. I glanced at Ty. He was several yards away, far enough, in the busy store, to be unaware of the question.

"He's my grandson," I said. I had neither the time nor the inclination to explain that this was my eldest grandchild, my only grandson, that I had held him in my arms when he was thirty minutes old, and that he would be puzzled at this question about his identity. But for an adult American it was a natural question, if a bit presumptuous. No harm intended.

Other questions and comments have been harder to brush off. "What does your father think," my daughter's neighbor asked her, "about the, um, situation?"—the "situation," apparently, being Ty's coffee-with-cream skin and dark brown eyes. A woman in our former church once referred to him as an "aborigine," and a man took note of Tyler's mixed ethnicity by referring to him, in my presence, as a "zebra."

These kinds of things leave me breathless with astonishment. I should be better prepared for these moments, I suppose. There are, after all, people who seriously propose turning the Northwest—where we now live—into an all-white territory, and my grandson is only half white. Under their scheme he would have to go. He's just not white enough.

Others insist that to be "authentic" Ty is obligated to adopt speech patterns, musical tastes, and attitudes that are supposedly black. According to this formula, apparently, Chuck D, whose rap performances have urged kids to kill cops, is a more authentic human being, a better role model for Tyler, than is James DePriest, the distinguished conductor of the Oregon Symphony, whose penchant for conducting music composed by "dead white guys" indicates to some that he is not black enough.

All this, of course, is nonsense. But it's hurtful nonsense. It makes people suspicious and fearful. It's divisive, and it has no place in the church or in the heart of the Christian.

Ethnic hostility is nothing new. The disciples were surprised to find Jesus talking to a Samaritan; they would not have done it. And later it took a direct and emphatic command from God to get Peter to enter the home of Cornelius, the Roman Gentile.

Paul addressed the issue in his letter to the church at Colosse. Having "put off the old [self] with his deeds," he wrote, and having "put on the new [self]," recognize that among followers of Jesus Christ "there is neither Greek nor Jew, circumcision nor uncircumcision, Barbarian, Scythian, [slave] nor free: but Christ is all, and is in all."

Let's remind ourselves here that the various peoples of the great Roman Empire did not belong to a mutual admiration society. Educated, sophisticated Greeks often looked down on the Jews as superstitious and xenophobic zealots. Jews, in turn, had a term of universal contempt and disgust for Greeks and other Gentiles: "uncircumcised dogs."

The "barbarians" were people from the northwestern corner of the empire, often fair-haired and blue-eyed, the people of my own distant ancestry. Urbane Romans considered these tribal people to be backward and ignorant. Scythians, who occupied part of the northeastern fringes of the empire, were even more exotic and strange. And there was a separate legal system for free citizens and the thousands of slaves.

But in Christ, Paul reminded members of the early church, all these distinctions must be put away. We have the Tyler Principle: we are family.

One Sunday after church my grandson asked a question that shocked me.

"Can brown boys," he wanted to know, "be missionaries?" I felt as if I had been stabbed in the heart with an icicle. The implications of his question were painful.

Did he somehow feel like a second-class citizen in his own church? Didn't the kids still sing, "Red and yellow, black and white?" And if they did, had he somehow still gotten the impression that he might be a second-class citizen in the Kingdom of heaven?

Perhaps he had. Certainly nobody had said it, or even intended it. But he had been told on his preschool playground, "We're not playing with you; you're a nigger." And in a mostly white church in a mostly white city, he had seen—as I had not—that most depictions of missions showed fair-skinned people talking, dark-skinned people listening. He had to wonder if he could play too.

Apparently others were more alert than I. I've been pleased to see that more recent pictures published by Christian presses show a variety of complexions. I'm sure that Jesus is pleased, too—quite likely brown-eyed, olive-skinned Jesus, if that matters to anyone.

I hope it does not. For all those washed in the blood of the Lamb there is only one color, the color of righteousness, the color of family. Call it God's Tyler Principle.

Endure Hardness as a Good Soldier
October 2007

"There they are," someone in the crowded bleachers said. "Off there to the right." And there they stood, nearly six hundred of our young men, maybe three hundred yards away, motionless ranks in the California sun.

The new Marines stood at the end of the long parade deck, an area off limits to the graduation day visitors because, explained a smiling Marine tour guide, "We're Marines—and you're not."

The Marine band struck up "The Stars and Stripes Forever," and the khaki and blue ranks swept forward, drill instructors marching alongside, bare swords cocked along powerful right arms, the red white and blue and the flag of the Corps leading on.

On they came, on they came. Then a command, and they halted, eyes straight ahead. Perfect silence. And then "Lehh—Hayh!" and the troops executed a left face, and there in the front row was Ty, straight as a rifle barrel, motionless as stone.

This was not the kid with the easy grin we had seen off at the Portland airport thirteen weeks earlier. Thirteen weeks of difficult, often painful training had turned Tyler into a strong, disciplined United States Marine, a man not to be taken lightly.

The Corps had sent us a DVD explaining the training regimen, from the minute a yelling drill instructor harried the recruits off the bus until the day when, after a final test called The Crucible, the exhausted, filthy young men stood before their instructor who now shook their hand, congratulated them, and pinned to their chest the globe and anchor acknowledging their new status as United States Marines.

Thirteen weeks of running, marching, jumping into a swimming pool in full dress and combat boots, rappelling down a three-story wall, being herded into a room and ordered to remove gas masks as stinging, strangling white vapors swirled around them, going at each other with pugil sticks and boxing gloves. Day after day of running, pushups, sit ups.

And finally The Crucible. Fifty-four hours in the field with little sleep and a total of three small meals, miles of hiking with heavy packs, of dragging heavy dummies under barbed wire through soupy mud, of carrying simulated wounded men on stretchers until hands and forearms became paralyzed. And at three o'clock on the final morning dashing up a steep hill in the dark, yelling in triumph.

Sixteen months later in Afghanistan the benefits of all this became plain. When Tyler had been ordered to Twenty-Nine Palms, California, for desert training there was little doubt about his next stop. And sure enough, he became part of the "surge," one of the 30,000 troops the military said would be needed to turn the tide in Afghanistan.

    He came home on leave for a week, and then one morning I drove him to the Portland airport. His sweet girlfriend Leah came, too. None of us said much. We parked, went inside, found a table near the concourse, sipped smoothies, and waited.

    Finally he looked at his watch, tossed the unfinished smoothie into a trash can, picked up his heavy sea bag, and moved into line. An official came over to him, ushered him past the civilian passengers, and led him to a quick security check. Tyler looked back once, grinned, and swung off toward the loading gate and was gone.

    Leah turned her face into my chest, crying softly. "This is hard," she said.

    "It is," I said. "But you know, he's had the best training in the world."

    And then one skillet-hot day in Helmond Province Ty's patrol heard shots. He was slogging along under a tremendous load: full pack, forty pounds of Kevlar body armor, five-pound helmet, M16-A4 assault rifle with 180 rounds, and the heavy barrel to a 240B machine gun with 240 rounds for it— roughly 110 pounds of gear, weapons and ammunition. The men threw up a perimeter, then moved toward an abandoned building. "Get up in the building!" Staff Sergeant Caughey yelled. "Move! Move! Get to the roof!"

Ty and the other men dashed into the building. He ran up two flights of stairs with all his gear, his weapons and over four hundred rounds of ammunition. "It was pretty much a sprint," he told me later.

Caughey shouted, "Get the gun up!" and in moments the Marines were in position. Soon the firing died down, and the men came down off the flat roof and moved back to the nearby base. Their dash to the roof, laden as they were, was an amazing feat of strength and discipline. But they had been prepared. They'd had the best training in the world.

Two thousand years ago James began his epistle to the early believers with a startling command. His readers were under heavy pressure from the pagan culture surrounding them, and from often hostile Jewish leaders. Their lives were not easy. But James counseled them to "count it all joy" when they encountered various testings.

How could that attitude be possible? Because, James went on, "the testing of your faith worketh patience," or endurance.

Paul admonishes believers to "endure hardness" as good soldiers of Jesus Christ. That toughness does not come from lying in a hammock drinking lemonade.

Marine training is demanding, even exhausting, but the Corps knows there will come a day when its troops will need to sleep on cold ground in a dust storm. "I've got grit in my ears, in my nose, in my mouth," Ty told us once on a brief phone call. "I've got grit just about everywhere you can have it."

They will need to stay alert when they haven't had much sleep. They will carry heavy loads. They will, if they mean to stay alive, have to act quickly and decisively.

It's natural to want to be comfortable, to want our days to pass peacefully. And it's easy to feel sorry for ourselves when trials come, maybe even to wonder if God loves us after all.

But Scripture tells us we are in conflict with a powerful and cunning adversary. "Did we in our own strength confide," Martin Luther wrote, "our striving would be losing," a caution to keep in mind when we encounter the testings that will make us strong.

Every drill sergeant barking orders knows what the recruits are going through, because he went through it. He also knows, better than the boys, why they must endure the hard things he makes them do. They have a great commission, a noble duty, and they must be strong to do it.

Scripture reminds us that our Great Captain was tested in every way that we are. He knew hunger and thirst, knew the hatred of those who opposed Him, knew the sting of betrayal. His life was difficult. And He was so strong a tomb could not keep him.

Those smooth talkers telling folks that God wants them to be rich and happy could not be more wrong. He wants us to be strong, to be good soldiers.

There's great honor in that—and in the end, great reward.

Saying It Our Way

How come, comedian and author Chris Rock once asked, how come the guy who scores a touchdown always says, "Hi, Mom"? How come nobody grins at the camera and says "Hi" to Dad?

After all, Rock went on, it's probably Dad who has made the monthly house payment, kept the lights on, and stocked the fridge.

"And what does Daddy get?" Rock asked rhetorically. "The big piece of chicken. Maybe."

I doubt that Dad minds. We fathers are pleased to have our children acknowledge their debts to their mothers, our wives who have worked hard and patiently to help bring our kids to maturity. We know, more than our sons do, what enormous investments in time, labor and prayer the boy's mom has poured out on him.

If Dad is at the game—and he probably is—he'll wait for the television crews to disappear, wait some more for his son to shower and dress, and the two men will bump fists, maybe share a brief embrace, and head for a steak. If the younger man is walking a little crooked after the high-speed pounding of an hour of football Dad might say, "You okay?" and his son will say, "Yep. Kinda hungry."

This is male code, and here's what it means:

"I'm proud of you, son, and thrilled by what you did out there. You were a man. I respect you and love you."

"Thanks, Dad. I'm grateful for your approval, and grateful for that first ball you gave me for Christmas, grateful for showing me how to hold it, how to put my thumbs together and make a basket with my hands to catch it, grateful for the hours you spent throwing passes to me when you had already put in a day's work and probably wanted to sit down and read the paper. I'm grateful for you sitting in the rain watching eighth grade football games. I'm glad you're proud of me. That's very important to me. I respect you and love you."

All this in a fist bump, the briefest embrace, and five words?

Yep.

Not much drama for a television audience, but then neither father nor son wants this exchange to appear on television. Except for entertainers (including religious ones), the genuineness of whose displayed emotions is in question, few American men want an audience for their deepest feelings.

It used to be fashionable to assert that this reticence was a sign that millions of American men were emotionally repressed, unable to feel or at least incapable of expressing their feelings, so they were chronically angry, worked too long, drank too much.

Rubbish.

American men know perfectly well how to express their regard and affection for one another and for our children, and we do it all the time, though we don't want to go on Oprah and talk about it in front of her, the production crew and an audience of millions. In brief, we are not drawn to public emotional nudity.

It's more likely that we will express our love through action. Women do this too, of course. For most of us there came the day when we understood that the aromatic breakfasts, fragrant rolls, gleaming tubs and shining floors of our childhood homes were ways that Mom was saying she loved us.

But Dad's efforts on our behalf may have been less visible, less directly realized.

Poet Robert Hayden understood only in his own adulthood the meaning of his father quietly discharging "love's austere and lonely offices":

Sundays too my father got up early
and put his clothes on in the blue black cold,
then with cracked hands that ached
from labor in the weekday weather made
banked fires blaze...
[and when he] had driven out the cold...
polished my good shoes as well.

I will be blunt but brief in speaking of my former son-in-law's failures as a father. He had no good example growing up of a loving, faithful father. Predictably, he wasn't much of an improvement as a dad, and I have served, for most of my eldest grandchild's life, as both grandfather and father. It wasn't an ideal situation for Ty or for me. Boys need both fathers and grandfathers—the roles and duties are complementary, not synonymous—but Dad was rarely around, and I was.

Tyler was sometimes short-changed, I know. When I was forty it was fun to fire passes to Ty's uncle Andy. For several years Andy and I played on the same softball team. But eventually, inevitably, my arm ached, my legs were gone, and playing ball was no fun. Besides, I was simply no good anymore. I was too old.

At age sixty I was not eager to take Tyler to the

batting cages. And I'd pick up a football, toss it from hand to hand, and know if I tried to throw it hard my shoulder would ache all night. And over the years my work responsibilities had increased. I didn't have a lot of time for baseball or fishing.

But there were trade-offs. Proverbs observes that the glory of an old man is his gray head. I had that, and the experience and increased knowledge that came with it.

And we found ways to spend time together. He had some musical talent, and my wife and I shivered through more November marching band performances than we would have if the big fellow whomping the bass drum, keeping the band on tempo, hadn't been ours.

When I was asked to speak at a camp in Idaho, Ty came along. He had recently obtained his learner's permit and needed to log some hours, so for most of the 500 miles he drove and we talked.

We spent the night in Baker City and visited the Oregon Trail Museum. We walked along the ruts still worn in the surface of the high desert, and looked across the wide valley at the steep rise of the Blue Mountains and talked about what it must have been like for the emigrants of 1850 to have struggled here after five months and 1,800 miles on the trail, and then to have seen those looming mountains, and about the kind of courage and determination it took to press on, on through the high pass, down the steep western slope, and along the big wild river another 250 miles to Oregon City.

We were glad for our air-conditioned Taurus, and glad of our comfortable hours together, man and growing boy.

It wasn't always comfortable, of course. There were curfews, chores, study expectations, not always received gladly. But we kept at it, this process of maturation.

And now the growing boy is a man. As I write he is stationed in Camp Lejeune, a continent away from his grandmother's table, from his grandfather's instructions.

"Have you seen Tyler's Facebook page?" my wife asks me.

"No. I didn't know he had one."

"Well," she says, "he does. And the picture he put on it is of the two of you together at his graduation from boot camp."

It's a simple picture: two men, an old teacher and a young Marine, walking and talking together, an old hand on a strong young shoulder.

    We both know what it means.

Out of the Ivory Palaces
2009

Seeing a child off to war must be as difficult a goodbye as humans know.

I suppose, if we had been making a sentimental movie, there would have been an overlay of weeping violins. There would have been close-ups of my grandson's handsome face. Perhaps there would have been stirring lines to deliver.

But the real thing wasn't like that at all. There were no violins, only the sounds of early traffic on I-5 at 4:30 in the morning. We were headed toward Portland International Airport, Tyler and I, and Leah, his girlfriend. Our sleep had been short, and mine, at least, had been thin, eroded by sadness and anxiety. We were tired, and looked it, and nobody said much.

We had known for months, since Ty, a Lance Corporal in the U.S. Marines Reserves, had been activated and posted to Twenty-Nine Palms in California for desert training: he was about to become part of the 30,000 troop surge bound for Afghanistan.

Those expectations were now official orders, and after a week's leave at home it was time for him and the other men in his unit of combat engineers to take a long journey in their country's service, a journey to a harsh, unpleasant place, far from the homes where they were loved, where their place at the table was one of honor, love and joy.

They were exchanging their warm homes, shaded yards and private bedrooms for Spartan military quarters, their orderly, prosperous communities for dusty towns and bleak villages whose inhabitants at best ignored them, at worst plotted to kill them.

When Tyler's unit arrived at Camp Leatherneck the air conditioning was out, and the men lay on the bare concrete floor to try to stay cool enough to sleep. They sometimes trudged for miles under a withering sun. They sometimes slept on cots under the sky, or even in the dirt, a whistling wind blowing powdery grit down their necks and into their ears and the corners of their eyes. Moon dust, they called it.

By November the wind was cutting cold. At home people were wrapped in cozy blankets at football stadiums with their friends, eating hot dogs, sipping hot coffee and looking forward to Thanksgiving.

That Thanksgiving our home, with thousands of others, included an empty chair. Thousands of us—wives, brothers, sisters, parents and grandparents—had seen our young men off in the past year, off to months of discomfort, stress and danger. For us at home this meant days, weeks, months of missing their presence, of news stories of Allied and American casualties, of knowing that our own young men could be part of the next report of the maimed and killed.

Some evenings my usually cheerful, chatty wife would fall silent for a long time, and I didn't need to ask why. I didn't want to talk about it either, the thing we were both thinking about, and had been all day.

At the same time we were proud of Tyler, proud of his willingness—his choice—to leave behind all that was his, the orchards and fields of Oregon, its clean streams and cool mountains, his friends, his sweet and beautiful girl, his family, to serve his country, to set aside his own comfort and safety for the sake of a high calling.

I understood all this, of course, that morning on the way to the airport. I was proud of my grandson, of course. Of course I appreciated what he was doing.

Still. As he was ushered through the check-in line for military passengers and disappeared down the concourse I had a heavy heart. Leah leaned on me, crying softly. "This is hard," she said. "It is," I said.

By Christmas Ty was home. He still had both legs and both arms, and his face was unmarked. But there was damage. He was tense, withdrawn, distracted. He wasn't sleeping well. He suffered from evil dreams.

My friend Terry is a psychologist who does a good deal of work with the military. "These guys haven't slept well for a long time," she told me. "They live with hyper-vigilance, one eye half open, on alert even when they sleep."

There was a price to be paid for Ty's good service. But when I asked him if he would volunteer again, knowing then what he knew now, he didn't hesitate. "I would," he said.

He's sleeping better now, the bad dreams diminishing, his jokes and quick laugh once again part of his conversation. For many other troops and their families the price has been far higher.

The apostle John wrote in his first epistle, "In this was manifested the love of God toward us, because that God sent his only begotten Son into the world, that we might live through him. Herein is love, not that we loved God but that he loved us, and sent his Son to be the propitiation for our sins" (1 John 4:9-10).

I won't pretend that I have the faintest idea of what that sending must have been like. I do know that God experiences grief, and sending his Son into a world generally indifferent, often hostile, finally murderous, must have been searing.

"Out of the ivory palaces," says the old song, "into a world of woe."

Woe from the beginning: a painful journey to Bethlehem for his young mother, the subject of gossip in her home town, a delivery with no professional medical care, a feed bin for the baby's first bed.

And later a flight to Egypt to escape the mass murder of toddlers. And a hard life: years without a home, "no place to lay his head"; the ingratitude of healed lepers; the hate of important, powerful men; and finally betrayal, abandonment and crucifixion. A high price.

But for us, who desperately needed help, "glad tidings of great joy," a Savior born in the city of David, the Lamb of God who takes away the sins of the world.

In the midst of music, lights and feasting, in our joy in the season of gifts, let's not forget the price of this one.

Homecoming

December 2009

We had been waiting for months, and now they were here. The headlights of buses carrying the members of Co. A Sixth Engineer Support Battalion swept across the wide parking lot of the Springfield, Oregon Armory and homed in on the building where hundreds of people—girlfriends, wives, small children, parents and grandparents—waited.

The buses huffed to a stop, the doors clunked open, and lean young men emerged.

What followed was a pure fountain of rejoicing. Wives and sweethearts called out to their men, and opened their arms wide. One young wife held out a baby for her husband to hold for the first time.

My grandson, Tyler, hugged his teary mom, then swept his grandmother into his powerful arms and kept her there for a long time. Neither said a word. There were no words for this flood of relief and joy, and they weren't necessary anyway.

Then he grinned at me and wrapped me in a

bear hug that threatened to crunch a vertebra or two. "It's good to see you, son," I managed.

"It's good to be here," he said.

I'd learn later, in terse snippets, about the hardships of military duty in Afghanistan—the blazing summer days, the cutting winds of winter, the dirt, the wind storms that blew fine, gritty "moon dust" into the men's quarters, their food, and their ears and eyes. The bullet that whipped past Ty's neck so close he felt the puff of its small, deadly wind. Exhaustion so complete that he dozed off on his feet.

All this I learned over the next few months, a little at a time. On this evening the anger and fear and dirt of a combat zone was set aside.

I looked around the Armory's big assembly room at the laughing people, bubbling with elated love. "So this is what it must be like," I said to myself.

I was thinking about what Jesus had said about the joy in heaven over even one sinner who repents, who leaves behind the road to death and comes to the house of life, the house of love, a house where his Father has been waiting for him.

The tough troops we welcomed home were hardly faultless. I'm certain some had teased a sister 'til she cried. I'm sure many had disobeyed parents, frustrated at least one teacher, maybe cheated on a school assignment, had come home past curfew, left a mess in the kitchen for Mom to clean up, told a lie or two. No doubt some had been written up for speeding, and a few for something worse. These were, after all, Marines, testosterone-turbocharged young men who were attracted to risk and challenge.

I'm also sure of this: on that night, the night the troops came home, nobody cared about any of that. Sibling quarrels, marital spats, parental frustrations and exasperations were not topics of discussion, not on the agenda. They just did not matter. They didn't even register. They were simply gone, "as far as the east is from the west," vanished, evaporated without so much as a thin residue left behind.

Sinners come home, I thought, *are not welcomed into heaven grudgingly.* They aren't expected to take off their muddy boots before they're allowed in. Their faults and shortcomings are not reviewed. There's no time for that, and no interest. The fatted calf is turning on the spit, and the band is playing.

In the Springfield Armory after the cries of joy and the shouted names, after the hugs and the tears, there were wide platters piled high with thick sandwiches, and tubs of ice chilling bottles of water and soft drinks. "Are you hungry, Ty?" I asked.

He was, but he was tired, too. It had been a long, long journey from Afghanistan to a base in Uzbekistan, then to Germany, then to Portland, and then a two-hour bus ride south along I-5 to Springfield. Could we maybe go to a quiet restaurant?

Of course we could, anywhere he chose.

At P.F. Chang's we loaded a long table with plates of egg rolls and lettuce wraps and lemon chicken and Kung Pao chicken and fat noodles and fried rice and barbecued pork and Mongolian beef. Ty's girl, Leah, was there, and her brother Luke, and her parents. A couple from the table behind us and the family to our left joined us in a toast to our young Marine, his war behind him.

I don't remember what the bill was. I know it wasn't cheap—and it didn't matter. Tyler mattered, and here he was, sharing our table once again.

My uncle, part of a tank crew in WWII, once reminded me bluntly, "War is smashing things up and killing people."

With no wish to sound melodramatic, I suspect that most of us welcoming our young men home felt as though this was a little like getting them back from the dead. It was a profound joy to see them, touch them, to set good food before them, to know that tonight they would sleep in safe, quiet rooms, and tomorrow would travel the roads of home without, in Tyler's words, "crossing my fingers hoping I wouldn't get blown up."

Perhaps our dinner that night was a hint of the celebratory feast John spoke of in his Revelation, our wars behind us, the heat and peril and weariness over, a restless dream from which we have awakened.

"They shall hunger no more, neither thirst anymore," the heavenly Father says of those He will at last welcome home.

I believe the night the boys came home I caught a glimpse of what heavenly joy must be like, and had a small taste of the celebration at the wedding feast of the Lamb.

It was enough to sharpen my anticipation for the Real Thing.

Big Mike

For many years, in addition to my work at Corban University, I taught evening classes at the Oregon State Correctional Institution. "What's that like?" people often asked. "Is it scary?"

The answer is no. Or, rather, hardly ever. Most of my students were bright, they certainly had time to study, they were generally cooperative, and, unlike teachers in many high schools and some universities, I knew that my students were not carrying guns.

I said hardly ever. There was "Fred," with his strange stare and crazy laugh, a guy whose unexpected bursts of laughter seemed to puzzle the other inmates. I never let him behind me. He eventually got out on parole and was killed in a fight with police.

And there was Mike Simeral, big, bad and angry. He enrolled in a course on poetry I was teaching, and he didn't take to it right away. One night early in the course he blew into the classroom like a blast of rainy Oregon wind, banged his big, hard bulk into a front row seat, and announced loudly his low opinion of our reading material.

This did not strike me as an inviting moment for debate. I ignored his challenge and just went on with the evening's study, a good strategy, I think. This was, after all, someone the other men seemed to treat carefully.

And with good reason. Mike had done five months in Unit 5, isolation, "the hole," for bashing in the side of another inmate's face with one punch, someone he had nothing against personally. He had done it for money—$150.

Mike soon settled down and became a good student, whose questions and comments proved him to be an alert and astute reader.

And then something happened that I would never have dared to imagine, and that—to my discredit—I had never even prayed for. Mike Simeral, big, bad, dangerous Mike, lingered after class. He had something to tell me. "I'm following the Lord," he said simply and quietly.

I had learned to be skeptical of jailhouse conversions. All too frequently they preceded a scheduled parole hearing.

But I had never known Mike to try to con

anybody. That was never his style. Intimidation and violence had been his forté. Con jobs were for weaker people.

I knew Mike was telling the truth. He looked different. His big tough mug had softened. His eyes had lost their angry challenge. And he sounded different. His voice had softened and quieted.

He offered the most unusual testimony of God's transforming power that I had ever heard. "I know this is real," he told me. "I don't want to hurt nobody no more. I used to like it—and I was good at it."

Later Mike told me that he had actually become a Christian before entering OSCI, but only lately, after working with the prison chaplain, had he made a complete break with his old life.

When he came to OSCI, by his own admission Mike still had "a big chip on my shoulder," a chip he'd been wearing for a long time. When Mike was ten, his father was killed in a logging accident. The day after the closed-casket funeral the sad angry boy went to the city swimming pool and took an axe to the wooden bleachers.

His mother remarried. Mike's stepfather was a violent alcoholic who beat both the boy and the woman.

When he was thirteen Mike was sent to a series of youth homes and juvenile detention facilities for a string of car thefts and burglaries.

In his sophomore and junior years of high school he was an outstanding wrestler, but his senior year he again did time for burglary. The years to follow were marked by repeated crimes that included fighting with the police, and finally the authorities had had enough of Mike Simeral. He was sitting in the county jail waiting for sentencing for a series of crimes that might have meant 105 years in prison.

At the county jail Mike was the "kingpin," the toughest of the tough, a thug who, if he felt like it, took the other inmates' suppers and dared them to resist. He finally was kept in a cell by himself most of the day.

One night he was allowed into the commons to read the paper. Lying on the newspaper was a tattered Good News Bible. "I threw it across the room," Mike recalls, "and threatened anyone who might put it back." He took the paper back to his bunk, read it, and when he came back out found the Bible back on the table. For some reason he took it back to his cell.

What happened next Mike remembers with crystal clarity. The bad man began to pray. "You know, God," he said, "I have no idea who You are or if You even exist. But I know there must be something better than this." He opened the ragged Bible to the Psalms and began to read. "The Lord is my light and my salvation…"

Big Mike began to weep. "I don't know who You are," he prayed, "but if You will show me and teach me what I should do, I'll follow You the rest of my life." He read on: "The Lord is my shepherd, I shall not want… He leadeth me beside the still waters, He restoreth my soul…"

And for the first time in his life the angry, violent man felt peace. "The Lord took a pressure off me," Mike says.

The next day Mike stood before a judge and heard his sentence: twenty-five years with a twelve and half year minimum.

Eight and a half years later, about to be released on parole, Mike looked out the window of his cell and admitted to himself that he was scared. He had no job, no clear plans. He turned to the Lord. He prayed simply, "You lead, I'll follow."

And that's what happened. Mike began his own home remodeling and repair business, Rebirth Maintenance, and then became a partner with his pastor in a business replacing lights in high places, such as those in parking lots and car dealerships. Not long after that the pastor gave Mike the keys to the equipment and said, "Here. It's all yours."

Mike is married now, and he and his wife are active in their church and in a ministry to the homeless. They haul their barbecue equipment down to the banks of the Willamette River, grill hot dogs and burgers, serve them on buns donated by a local grocer, and tell the eager eaters that Jesus is the One Who satisfies all their hungers.

"If the Lord can change me," Mike says, "He can change anybody. He doesn't say 'Clean yourself up,' He says 'Come to Me just the way you are.' There's no sin so great that God won't forgive us."

Last summer a prison guard recognized Mike at a baseball game. He came over to shake the big man's hand. "Bull!" he said, using Mike's prison nickname. "How are you?"

Mike smiled. "Bull is dead," he said. "Michael is alive and well, walking with God."

Tony Giacoletti

I was reading a story on security at Oregon airports when my eyes strayed into the next column, the obituaries. "Tony Giacoletti," the name read. I was so startled I nearly dropped the newspaper. Could there be more than one Tony Giacoletti in Salem, Oregon? "September 26, 1963—January 9, 2002." That would be right for the Tony I knew.

And then the brief biography: "Tony Giacoletti, 38, died Wednesday of a brain aneurysm.

"His occupation was fisherman/carpenter, and he was a past student of Western Baptist Bible College [now Corban University]. He loved riding his Harley..."

I always knew when Tony was arriving for classes. I could hear his big bike rumbling and snorting up the road onto campus. He'd wheel into a motorcycle-sized parking space, stomp down the kickstand, lift off his helmet and run a big hand through his shaggy brown hair.

Tony was not the poster boy for a conservative Christian college fastidious about its image. He was big—probably 6'3" in his socks, taller in his heavy black biker boots—and rough. His thick hair was carelessly cut, and too long to be in compliance with the dress code spelled out in the Student Handbook. In his riding leathers he would not be a welcome sight striding down the sidewalk toward you after dark.

Tony was a new Christian, and he seemed refreshingly unaware of the details of a safe Christian image. He had other things to work on. One was his temper. He stayed around one day after class to tell me how much he was learning and growing. "I've asked the Lord to help me with my temper, Mr. Hills," he said. Silently noting Tony's dimensions once again, I hoped that his prayers were being answered.

It turned out that they were. "And I know He's helping me," Tony went on. "Last week I only said '_____!' once."

I confess to being startled at the candor and detail of Tony's report. This was not the kind of thing I had ever hear at a Wednesday night "testimony" session. He had not intended to discomfit me, I knew, or even been aware that he might. He was simply a man without guile, a man of humble heart, measuring his growth as a child might, with a kind of pencil mark on the wall.

If his problem with his temper continued, I never saw it. The Tony I knew was eager to listen, slow to speak, a gentle, soft-spoken man.

But not all his baggage was so successfully displaced. A couple of months ago I was pleased and surprised to see him in church. Tony had moved, and I had lost track of him. I almost didn't recognize him. He had started to lose his hair, and in typical straightforward fashion clipped what was left nearly down to his scalp. And he looked weary and a bit eroded.

"Mr. Hills," he said, and I knew the soft voice.

"Tony! It's been a long time. It's good to see you again. How are you?"

"Well," he said, "I've made some mistakes. My walk hasn't always been what it should be, but I'm back in here in Salem, and I'm gonna be attending this church." And then he introduced me to the friend he had brought along, a man whose careful, cramped eyes suggested that he too had seen some difficult days.

Tony didn't have a problem with his temper any longer, and hadn't had for years. But he still battled the bottle, and sometimes he lost. He offered no excuses for his episodes of heavy drinking, nor did he shrug them off as of little consequence. "Pray for me," Tony said. Billy Sunday, who used to be a heavy drinker, said that after he gave his heart to Jesus Christ he could "pass the saloon in my strength and not have a desire to take a drink, but there are many who cannot."

Tony was one of those who sometimes could not. I don't know why God removed the desire for alcohol from one man and not another, or why Tony could go without a drink for a long time and then fall off the wagon. But I do know this. Tony cared for drunks and addicts and misfits. He understood them in ways that I cannot. He took care of them when their addictions and compulsions overwhelmed them.

As he once explained to me about someone he was caring for, "If I didn't take care of him, he would die. I clean him up when he's sick. It don't bother me. I make sure he eats and that he's in bed at night."

And he told him about Jesus. As the obituary noted, "He pointed many to Jesus Christ along his walk."

Perhaps it is worthy of note that Tony was a fisherman and a carpenter. As I read the obituary once again I couldn't help but reflect that Jesus, the carpenter from Nazareth, understood and loved big rough men whose weaknesses were there for all to see. "Follow me," He said to them, "and I will make you fishers of men."

Tony Giacoletti, warts and all, took Him at His word.

Beside the Still Waters

Summer 2003

"Sergeant Shoemaker," Sergeant Daniel Frey said, "how are we gonna get out of here? Which way is home?"

Staff Sergeant Willie Shoemaker was in charge of a squad of combat engineers who had been laying concertina wire and mines in a meadow two miles outside Monschau during the Battle of the Bulge. Just before sundown they had come under artillery fire—air bursts that exploded in the treetops, sending hot shrapnel and jagged pieces of wood whizzing through the meadow. The men ran through the snow to their trenches in the woods, where they crouched in the cold earth, waiting out the bombardment. Finally, when it was dark, the Germans stopped firing.

But this area was unfamiliar to Shoemaker and his men, and in the deep darkness—nobody shines a light in a combat zone—neither he nor his men had the slightest idea of how to get out of the trees and find the road back to the American positions at Monschau.

If they went the wrong way, they could blunder into the German lines and be captured or killed. If they stayed where they were, they might be overrun.

This wasn't the first time in this war that Willie Shoemaker's life had been on the line. He and his group of combat engineers had been in the first assault wave on D-Day, June 6, 1944. Their job then was to clear a fifty-foot-wide path through the obstacles and mines at the Easy Green sector of Omaha Beach, "bloody Omaha," so that the troops and tanks could come ashore. After six hours of being bashed about in the stormy English Channel—"Men were seasick, and the landing craft next to us sank; three tanks went down, but I think the men were saved," Shoemaker recalls—the clumsy landing craft headed toward the beach. It was 6:30 in the morning when, in Shoemaker's words, "the first miracle" occurred.

The boat in front of them hit a sandbar and couldn't get off. Shoemaker's boat moved ahead of the stranded craft and plowed toward Omaha Beach a minute and a half ahead of schedule, ninety seconds that probably made the difference between survival and annihilation.

The ramp on the landing craft banged down and

Sergeant Shoemaker led his squad onto the beach. "There were no footprints when we got there," he remembers. German troops on the bluff above the beach were firing on them, but resistance was not yet in full force.

"I only lost two men." Shoemaker speaks a little slower now, a little quieter. "Morgan and Little Brandt. They went down at the same time, about ten feet from me. Morgan was hit by a machine gun round. Little Brandt had a heart attack. He was unmarked. His medical records showed that he'd had a heart condition since childhood, but he'd been drafted anyway."

Shoemaker's squad quickly set their charges and fixed their detonator cord. "The frogmen—they call 'em SEALS now—blew up the obstacles in the water," Shoemaker recalls, "and then we blew up the obstacles on the beach—cleared that fifty-foot path. Then it was time to take cover.

"Now here's the miracle. A German heavy machine gun started sweeping back and forth across Easy Green, plowin' up the beach. If we'd got there a minute and half later like we were supposed to, we'd probably all have been killed. I believe the Lord was watching out for me."

Sergeant Shoemaker and his men spent two days clearing the mines and obstacles from Omaha Beach and then moved inland with the Allied cavalry and infantry. They cleared minefields, laid temporary bridges, and cut roads for trucks and tanks, moving through France toward Belgium, increasing pressure on the western front as the Red Army advanced toward Germany from the east.

Some German officers recognized the inevitable end and favored surrender before their country was destroyed. But Hitler—hoping to split the Allied armies and perhaps buy time until his new weapons (the first missiles and the first jet planes) might at the last minute change the war's outcome—launched one final, desperate attack.

On the morning of December 16, 1944, Nazi panzers and infantry slammed into the thinly-held Allied lines in the Ardennes Forest. Bad weather kept the superior Allied air forces out of the fight, and for five days the Germans hammered a deep dent—the bulge—in the Allied lines. Before the great battle was over and the German army began its full and final retreat, Allied forces would suffer 70,000 casualties.

It was during this great struggle that Sergeant Shoemaker and his squad crouched in foxholes in the cold dark of a forest with no clear idea of how to get back to American positions in Monschau. Sergeant Frey's question hung in the air: "How are we gonna get out of here? Which way is home?"

"The Lord put the Twenty-third Psalm in my mind," Shoemaker recalls. "The words just popped into my head: 'The Lord is my shepherd; I shall not want. He maketh me to lie down in green pastures: He leadeth me beside the still waters'—and right there I said out loud, 'Yes!'"

"Sergeant Shoemaker?" Frey said.

"Still waters," Shoemaker said. "I know how we're going to get out of here. Get right behind me and grab my belt. Have all the men line up and hold onto the man in front of him."

Sergeant Shoemaker had remembered the sound of snow melt trickling along the edge of the road that ran into the forest. That road led to the road to Monschau. The men moved out behind their sergeant, who soon, in the dark and quiet forest, picked up the faint sound of trickling water.

Back in Monschau, fed and in dry clothes, Shoemaker's men asked how he knew which way to go in the dark woods. "The Lord told me," Shoemaker said, "through the psalm."

"We don't have a sergeant," one of the men quipped, "we have a guardian angel."

Willie Shoemaker shook his head. "No," he said, "we have the Lord. Remember what General Eisenhower said before we headed to Normandy: 'Let us all beseech the blessing of the Almighty God.' The Lord took care of us."

By the time Germany surrendered in May of 1945, Willie Shoemaker had been given a battlefield commission and had been awarded a silver star for conspicuous courage in action. August of that year found him on a troop ship headed to Boston, where he was to be assigned to a combat unit being readied for an invasion of Japan.

"When we sailed into Boston harbor"—and here the old soldier flashes his 150-watt smile—"a fireboat came out to meet us. It threw water in the air, and there was a band playin'. Then a fella on that boat picked up a bullhorn. 'Welcome home, boys!' he shouted. 'Japan has surrendered. The war's over!'"

"When you're headed into combat," Willie Shoemaker says, "your mind is on the Lord." Over fifty years later it's plain to all who know this man that his focus has never changed.

Having the Time of Your Life

October 1995

"I'm scared," Ellen admitted as we paused between classes, enjoying the October sunshine.

"These kids are awfully bright, and I haven't been in school in over thirty years. I don't know if I can keep up."

Since her husband's sudden death several years earlier, Ellen had worked in a supermarket. The job offered security and decent money, enough for a widow to live on if she were careful. She worked hard, she was friendly, she was a good employee. She could keep doing this and take adequate care of herself until retirement and Social Security.

So what was she doing here? Why would a woman her age give up her home, her job, her insurance, her settled way of life, to move to a new city and enroll as a freshman in college?

Part of the answer, she told me, was physical. Hour upon hour of repetitive motion—bending to snatch up bags of flour and jugs of milk, running them over the scanner, then reaching to place them just so in the sacks—had given her a round-the-clock backache.

But there was more to her decision than sore muscles. "What I was doing just didn't seem to be enough anymore," she explained. "I didn't know exactly what I wanted to do, but I knew I wanted to work with people. And I wanted to do more for them than bag their groceries. I was ready for some kind of ministry."

And that, she knew, meant she had to get training—a lot of it. "So here I am," she said, smiling. "Scared to death, and having the time of my life."

And what a time she had. There were difficulties, to be sure. Money was tight. The hours were long. Some deficiencies in academic skills required extra attention and effort. But soon it became clear that God was blessing Ellen's courage, faithfulness, and hard work in specific ways.

Her academic performance earned her high marks, and her growing reputation as a woman of strength, wisdom, and high character brought to her students whose own struggles and fears prompted them to seek out someone like mom, someone who could offer guidance and reassurance.

Ellen's senior year the students elected her homecoming queen. At the reception after the big game, she held the place of honor. "Well," I said with a grin, "looks like you're having a good time."

She laughed. "Can you believe this? I'm having the time of my life."

Grandma is college homecoming queen

Statesman-Journal, Salem, Ore., Saturday, February 7, 1987, 3

By Hank Arends
Of the Statesman-Journal

Ellen Jacobs is a 53-year-old grandmother. She's also this year's homecoming queen at Western Baptist College.

She was presented as queen during half-time activities at the Friday night basketball game with Oregon Institute of Technology.

She was elected this week by the student body from an eight-member court, whose other members are all decades younger.

"I was so astounded when they nominated me as princess and then, when Professor Hills called my name (Thursday night), it took a second to sink in," she said. "I'm still floating four feet off the floor."

Jacobs, a junior at the Salem college, is to graduate in the fall with a bachelor's degree in psychology and a minor in business. She hopes to pursue a master's and obtain her doctorate before she's 60.

Jacobs was widowed a dozen years ago. She was born in Kent, Wash., and moved to Salem in 1984 from Auburn, Wash.

She said she finally tired of working in a grocery store. Deciding to go back to college, she checked out three institutions and liked Western best. She sold her home to move here but said she eventually ran out of money. She works part-time at J. K. Gill Stationers.

She has three daughters and five grandchildren in Auburn. One daughter, when told of her selection as queen, said she wanted a photo and program to post in the grocery where her mother had worked.

The 5-foot-3 Jacobs said she is accepted by other students at the college.

As an extravagance for her selection as queen, she said, she went out and bought an $89 off-white silk-and-lace gown.

Jacobs said she eventually would like to work at counseling women and teens in a church.

The local newspaper carried the story of the grandma campus queen. But Ellen's story was far from ended. She earned her bachelor's degree, went on to take a master's degree, served in women's ministries in a large church and went on to serve as head of the Family Ministries program in Corban University's Division of Professional Studies, a program designed especially for adult learners.

And there's the story of Alice, who devoted years to bringing up her children, doing it alone for a long time. When her boys were grown, she came to school, pursued her Biblical studies with a passion, and discovered a flair for writing. Then soon after she marched across the platform to receive her diploma, she boarded a plane for Thailand to teach English as part of a missionary work in Bangkok.

And then there's Rick, the big ex-highway patrolman with a bullet in his leg. He graduated—along with his daughter—and began full-time ministry as a pastor.

Ellen and Alice and Rick are among the growing numbers of mature Christians who have realized that God's call to ministry is not exclusively—or even primarily—directed to the young.

After all, Abraham and Moses were men of years when God called them for a specific purpose. The sons of Zebedee had an established fishing business; Barnabas was a prosperous businessman; Saul of Tarsus was an eminent scholar. In one way or another, they all asked the question Saul asked on his knees on the Damascus road: "What wilt thou have me to do?"

The answer may be, as it apparently was to Lydia, the seller of purple in the book of Acts, "Continue in your business where you are, and serve Me there."

But it may also be, "Arise and go." It's a very simple command, and there's no age restriction. If it's time to arise, wherever you are, and at whatever age, go. You'll have the time of your life.

Acquainted with Grief

At first I couldn't make out what Brenda was saying. Her eyes were swollen and red, and she choked on her words. And I was entirely unprepared for what she was trying to make me understand.

"You haven't heard? Nancy's dead."

"What? Who?"

"Nancy. Nancy Beers. She–she died."

I felt as if someone had dropped a brick of ice on my skull. Nancy? The only daughter of my friend Rich? The sister of the man Brenda would soon marry? Nancy was only twenty-three years old. She was only weeks away from celebrating her first wedding anniversary. She was expecting a baby in three months. I couldn't be hearing this. Tall, beautiful Nancy, the luminous young wife who smiled at everyone?

"Nancy Noland?" I said, using her familiar maiden name. "Rich's daughter?" Brenda nodded and burst into tears.

"Can you tell me what happened?"

"She went to the hospital three days ago," Brenda said. "She had been having headaches, bad ones, and she couldn't take her migraine medication because of the baby. And—and she died. I don't know why."

In a few days we had the medical reason: a very aggressive brain tumor, probably untreatable even if for some reason it would have been detected. It took Nancy and it took her unborn son, Rich and Peggy's first grandchild.

That was the medical reason. Four days later at a school memorial service for Nancy I stood before a silent group of students who, I knew, hoped I would offer a theological reason for the death of their friend. I didn't know. I still don't. Nobody knows but God.

In times like these, I think, asking why is of little use. Much better to ask what: What can we learn?

Christians are citizens of two countries, and we live with the tension of dual citizenship.

Sometimes this tension is *political.* Daniel and the three Hebrew friends, for example, had to defy the law of the emperor in order to obey the laws of God. And over the centuries many men and women have, like Peter and John, said to those in power, "Whether it be right in the sight of God to hearken unto you more than unto God, judge ye" (Acts 4:19).

But sometimes the tension is *emotional.* We are born into the world we know through our senses and experience. It is the world we were created to inhabit, love and tend before we brought a curse on it and on ourselves. And in spite of the damage done by the rebellion of the human race there is still much to love: sunlight and warm stones, the scent of new leaves on cottonwood trees, the smell of rain, the clean, cold streams of Oregon, cherry blossoms, oranges, my wife's warm smile and warm touch, the grace and speed of my son scoring from second base, my daughter's clear blue eyes. It's right that I love these things, and as a creature, one of the sons of Adam, it is hard to think about leaving them.

Yet, at the same time there is another country—the place of our eternal citizenship, the one the Bible tells us is "better." We believe this is so. But at a memorial for a young friend, daughter, and wife, things seem askew, the time "out of joint." As one of my friends once reminded me, we are Christians, not Stoics. We are, like our Savior, acquainted with grief.

"To everything there is a season," said the Preacher. There is a time to mourn.

For a season. At the grave of a loved one the loss

seems terribly permanent. Something mysterious and irrevocable has occurred. She will not come back tomorrow or next month or next year or—we say—ever. That's the view from here, where we measure our lives by heartbeats and sundowns and the phases of the moon.

But there is that other world, the one where God is the light, where the former things have passed away. We don't see well now. We stumble and grope along, in the Shadowlands, says C. S. Lewis, seeing in part and knowing in part. In time—or out of it—God promises we will see clearly and know as we are known.

But for now there is no answer to why. Job, battered by loss upon loss, ultimately had to confess his ignorance and cling to God's grace and wisdom. His friends advanced tidy explanations for Job's suffering, and were utterly wrong.

The rain falls on the just and the unjust, the righteous suffer as well as the wicked. But why this particular person? We don't know.

Better to ask what: what can we take away from our encounters with loss and sorrow?

Let me suggest one thing. The final scene in Thornton Wilder's *Our Town* is set in a cemetery on a hill overlooking the town, Grover's Corner. We hear the dead speak, and Emily Webb, a young mother who a few days ago died in childbirth, observes about her life—and ours—"It goes so fast. We don't have time to look at one another."

How would we treat a lost friend if, like Lazarus, she came back to us? If we had quarreled how long would it take us to apologize? Would it be hard to forgive her imperfections? Would we wait for her to do something for us or would we be eager to serve her?

What can we learn from grief and loss? Perhaps we can remember to look attentively at one another, to treat one another with the kindness and care we would offer if this were the last day we had together this side of heaven. It could be.

Saying goodbye from here is hard. We sorrow—but not without hope. Even in the midst of mourning we listen for the trumpet, when we shall be changed, when mortality will put on immortality, when we shall become, in the poet's words, "immortal diamond," and sorrow will be turned to joy.

At the Funeral of James Anderson

December 2002

James played football for South Salem High School when my three older children were there. He explained to me one day why he preferred playing defense to offense. Thick and squarish, James obviously was a lineman, and on offense he was sometimes expected to pull—to leave his post in the interior line, sprint to the outside and block for the ball carrier behind him. "How was I supposed to get out there faster than some little 180-pound running back?" he said. "I am not made for speed. But on defense I staked out my territory and hunkered down, and anybody that tried to run through there was gonna have a problem."

Those were the facts, and James respected facts. But, as I learned when he came to Corban University, if his feet were slow his mind was swift and agile. His mind did not hunker—it danced. I soon learned that, when the big fellow's hand went up, the class was about to become more interesting. His questions were thoughtful and provocative, his comments insightful.

Class was never over for James. Some students let you know that 48 of the allotted 50 minutes are up. They rouse from their daze, snap shut their notebooks with a sound like a whacked Ping-Pong ball, shuffle their feet, sigh, and in other ways show signs of life for the first time that hour. And the professor wonders why he didn't become a plumber—a useful, necessary and well-paid tradesman whose clients are always glad to see him.

One reason is that there are always a few James Andersons. For him the end of the class session did not signal that he was now free to play video games or troll for babes. It often meant that, since we had run out of classroom time before he ran out of questions, our discussion simply moved to the hall, the sidewalk or the lunch table.

It's assumed that good teachers make good students. No doubt that's sometimes true. I know for certain that good students make good teachers. I saw early on that James expected a lot out of me, as I did of him, expectations that I believe we both found energizing and invigorating.

One of the great rewards of what I do is that students sometimes become friends. We're interested in the same things, we've read the same writers, we have sharpened one another's iron; and after class and after commencement we still do.

Several years ago I was asked to write a series of short articles on the classic Christian virtues, one of which is compassion. I remembered something James had once said—that the inverse of compassion is not cruelty, it is indifference. Nazi death camp administrators didn't murder Jewish individuals because they had hated them, particularly, they just did not regard them.

I wasn't making as much headway on the article as I would have liked, and asked James to lunch so I could pick his brain. Over enchiladas he told me about his work at Hillcrest, a detention facility for young criminals. "They have very little understanding of how their actions affect other people," he told me. "It's my job to help them understand, and to care."

James cared. He cared about young people whose violent deeds shocked us and horrified us when we read about them in the newspaper. James was that rare human being who combined a cool head with a warm heart. He could maintain hope without harboring illusions, which meant he could be of good service to those that most others had no hope for.

James was not afraid of them, and he believed

that God's grace extended to robbers, rapists and murderers. He decided to go back to school—not to study English this time, but to earn a master's degree in social work. "I want to be in a position to help make policy," he told me. He had begun to stake out his territory.

That's not going to happen, now, and Oregon will be the poorer. We are all the poorer for James' absence. He was a strong presence, and it feels strange to think of him not being here, to observe the space that he would have filled with that wide, strong body, the silence in place of all that intelligent vitality.

Saying goodbye is a sharp grief—but not a permanent one. It's a grief for us, but James is fine. He is even now, I believe, confirming a number of hypotheses, revising some others, having some questions answered, heading off into some new territory.

On Eagles' Wings

Rain lashed the window of the commuter plane. "Ladies and gentlemen," the captain said, "please remain in your seats with your seatbelts fastened. This will be a bumpy flight."

The flight attendant slid into the seat next to my father, Carl Hills, and tightened her seat belt. "That's not encouraging," Hills said. "Those two guys across the aisle"—he nodded at Lee Webb and Willis Booth—"we crash landed yesterday at 5,000 feet."

She stared. "Nobody does that," she said, "and lives."

* * *

The three pastors were flying home from the 1964 GARBC National Conference in Des Moines. They planned to refuel in Salt Lake City and push on to the Bay Area. But over Nebraska thunder storms quickly brewed, air boiling up at 4,000 feet a minute, enough to fold a small plane's wings like tinfoil.

Lee Webb, piloting his four-seater Mooney, turned 180 degrees, radioed the airport in Grand

Island, and brought the plane down. The men ate lunch, went bowling, then about 1:00 checked the FAA weather report. They were given the go-ahead.

The plane lifted off toward Salt Lake City, but soon a big storm cell rose in the flight path. Webb flew around it. Then there were more. He had to dodge them, too, and before long was well off course.

He flew over a small airport, asked about landing. Not advisable, the tower answered. They were experiencing strong winds, thunder and lightning.

The men flew on. They studied a book of maps, and another showing airports and landing strips. Below lay nothing but ragged mountains. The fuel gauge fell steadily. Then—suddenly—a valley with a river running north to south. The Green River?

Maybe. Somewhere on the Green was Dutch John Dam, and near the dam the books showed a pair of landing strips. But—assuming this was the Green—was the dam north or south? Webb said, "Well, most of the time I was flying south around the storms. We'll head north." He didn't have to explain what was riding on his decision. They had twenty minutes of fuel.

He followed a dirt road north. They couldn't land on it, but it had to lead somewhere.

And then there was a big plateau, and on its flat

top a grassy landing strip. It had rained recently. The strip might be soft. Webb made one low pass to take a look—there wasn't enough fuel for another—circled into the wind, and came down into knee-high grass. The surface held, and the Mooney rolled to a stop.

The three men got out, thanked the Lord for the safe landing, and began hiking along a road toward a ranger station they had seen. They needed to let the FAA know where they were, and figure out what to do next.

A pickup truck rolled to a stop. "You guys got a problem?" the driver asked. He listened to the men's story. "There's a motel up ahead," he said, "but you won't get a room. Tomorrow's opening day on the Green River." He was a doctor from Salt Lake City, here to fish. He invited the three preachers to hop into the back of his pickup, drove to the motel, handed the men his truck keys, and pointed the way to Vernal, 35 miles away. They could find him on the river tomorrow.

On the way to Vernal the men saw a meadow through the trees. A small plane might—might—be able to land there.

The men found a room, and next morning drove to the airport and bought two five-gallon cans of fuel, enough to fly the plane to Vernal for refueling. They drove back to the plane, and while Webb poured the gas into the tank Hills and Booth took the truck back to where the doctor was fishing. The doctor drove the two back to the airstrip and said goodbye.

The weather was perfect, blue sky with a few puffy clouds, and Webb had the plane ready to go. He checked his instruments, taxied to the end of the strip, turned into the wind, increased RPM's and released the brake. The Mooney roared down the grassy strip—and then suddenly Webb backed off. "Something doesn't sound right," he said. He taxied back to the head of the strip and ran through his procedures again. Everything seemed fine. Once more he released the brakes, and halfway down the runway aborted again. "Something just doesn't seem quite right," he said, and wheeled back to the end of the strip once more. They were burning into their small fuel supply.

Webb blasted down the strip again, and flew out over the edge of the plateau, out over the valley far below. Suddenly the engine began to skip and pop. The stall buzzer bleated, signaling that the plane's airspeed was barely enough to stay aloft. Webb had to sacrifice altitude to gain enough speed to fly.

Now they were below the rim of the plateau, with

no way to get back to the strip. At the other end of the valley rose a high ridge. No way to get over that, either. Webb circled the valley. There were fences, cattle, big boulders, no place to put the plane down. They kept losing altitude.

"Fellas," Webb said, "I'm going to try to fly over that road to Vernal. Maybe we can follow it through the ridge." And with the engine still stuttering he turned to fly along over the road. The trees seemed to be rising toward them, and then the plane was below the treetops, following the winding road through the forest. Webb was standing the plane nearly on its wingtips as he yanked it through the tight curves.

The plane buzzed over a truck, wheeled through another curve, then another. And there before them loomed the big power lines carrying thousands of volts from the generators of Dutch John Dam.

Hills had been praying—aloud, it turned out—"Lord, help Lee fly this plane." Now he prayed, "Lord, you're gonna have to do more. You have to pick this plane up."

They were almost to the lines. And then suddenly a little thermal lifted them over the lines and up, up over the ridge.

And there below them lay the meadow. "I'm

gonna take it in," Webb said, and wheeled over the meadow. "What do you see down there, Carl?"

The near end was littered with windfalls and boulders. They would try the far end. Webb decided to crash land; he didn't want the landing gear to snag and cartwheel the plane. He shut down the engine to reduce the chance of fire. They hit the ground at about 75 mph, banging, scratching, screeching through sagebrush and over stones, and then the plane crabbed to the left and stopped. The men whipped off their seatbelts, bolted out the doors, and sprinted away. But there was no fire and nobody was hurt.

The men shook hands.

Lee said, "Sorry I couldn't talk to you there over the road. I was too busy."

"That's okay," Carl said. "I wasn't talking to you anyway."

The driver of the truck they had buzzed was running toward them, and others following him, and it was clear what three sermons would be about on Sunday.

The Seven Deadly Sins

The Seven Deadly Sins

In A.D. 590 Pope Gregory I issued a list of sins against which Christians should especially guard themselves. It was not the first such list. Proverbs, for example, names seven sins that God detests. But "the seven deadly sins" codified for the medieval church—and for our own—the nature of sinful thought, which will surely eventuate in sinful acts.

There are no laws against the seven deadly sins themselves; the best our legal system can do is try to restrain the behavior that works out of these crimes of the heart. Greed itself is not illegal, for example, but the frauds, thefts and robberies that greed provokes bring serious prison time.

But this is always after the fact. Jesus traces bad behavior back to a corrupt heart. He indicted the Pharisees for whitewashing a rotten interior, a tomb filled with "dead man's bones."

"The Seven Deadly Sins" expose the bones.

These articles—except "Lust"—published here for the first time, and the articles on the sins' antithetical virtues, were originally published by Regular Baptist Press.

Special thanks to Joan Alexander at RBP for proposing and editing the series.

Greed

The story in 1 Kings 21 has its comic elements. There's something laughable in the figure of a king, the richest and most powerful man in the country, whining and pouting like a child whose mother won't give him a piece of candy.

In this case, the candy is a vineyard that adjoins the palace property. Ahab wants it for an herb garden; Naboth owns it. King Ahab has offered to buy it, but the land has been in Naboth's family for years, and he doesn't want to sell. The vineyard is his livelihood and his children's inheritance. Any sensible person would understand immediately why he wanted to keep it.

But greed has nothing to do with common sense. Poor Ahab is so distraught that he can't eat his dinner. He goes straight to bed and turns away his face, too upset to deal with such cruel circumstances.

There's nothing funny, though, about the rest of the story. When Ahab's wife, Jezebel, hears what the trouble is, she promises to take care of things. And she does. She defames honest Naboth, hiring two "sons of

Belial" to publicly accuse him of blaspheming God and the king, and has him shamefully executed.

There is something crazy about all this, of course. A king allows himself to be so obsessed with a vineyard he doesn't need that he has a man killed for it? Well, greed is a kind of madness, a complete loss of any sense of economic purpose and proportion. Money is no longer seen for what it is, a means to an end—the provision of shelter, food and clothing—but becomes an end in itself.

A century and a half ago, a man went to the woods to conduct an experiment in living. Judging from the complaining and worrying that he so frequently heard in his hometown of Concord he concluded that "the mass of men lead lives of quiet desperation," and he aimed to show that such worry was unnecessary if only one would live more simply.

He built a small cabin, planted a garden and, for two years and two months, chronicled the days, weeks and months of his sojourn on the banks of Walden Pond. His name was Henry David Thoreau, and in essays titled "Where I Lived and What I Lived For" and "Economy" he explained that he "went to the woods to live simply," "to front the essential facts of life," and to be certain that, when he came to the end of his life, he would not "discover that I had not lived at all."

"The cost of something," Thoreau observed, "is the amount of one's life required to be exchanged for it." Since the "gross necessaries of life" were food, fuel, shelter, and clothing, the issue was how much of our lives we wished to exchange for more and richer food, a larger house, and clothing which was merely fashionable when last year's garments were still suitable. "If my coat is good enough to worship God in, it will do, will it not?" he asked. And finally: "Shall we always study to obtain more, and not sometimes be content with less?"

The greedy man is obsessed with obtaining more, always, always more, though he has no additional use for the "more" that he craves. In medieval literature the recurring image of the dragon in a cave coiled atop a heap of treasure pictures the obsessiveness and futility of greed, the deadly wakefulness in defense of something that is of no utility.

One thinks of the covetous schemers indicted by Micah: "Woe to them that devise iniquity, and work evil upon their beds! When the morning is light, they practice it... And they covet fields, and take them by violence; and houses, and take them away: so they oppress a man and his house" (Micah 2:1-2).

There is a link between this economic perversion of greed and other sins. To the greedy, nothing governs acquisition—not common decency, nor sacred trust, nor friendship. They are shameless in the pursuit of More. In Isaiah's words, they "beat...people to pieces, and grind the faces of the poor" (Isaiah 3:15).

Peter warns of those who may use even the office of prophet or teacher to exploit those who trust them: "Through covetousness shall they with feigned words make merchandise of you" (2 Peter 2:3). They have a heart "exercised with covetous practices," or in more contemporary language, they are masters in greed (2 Peter 2:14). Can anyone read this passage without thinking of the nearly round-the-clock telecasts of certain "ministries" whose programming is almost entirely given over to entertainment and requests for money?

And Judas, the embezzler—so greedy and hardhearted as to be unhappy when Mary anointed the feet of Jesus with spikenard rather than selling it and depositing the funds in the disciples' treasury where he could get at it—finally sold out his friend and Lord for thirty silver coins.

To guard against covetousness or greed, some

have taken vows of poverty. But this may miss the point. After all, the Bible is full of righteous people whom God made prosperous. Job, Abraham, and Barnabas come immediately to mind.

Thoreau's sojourn in the woods may not be appropriate for most of us. But his question is appropriate: "Shall we always study to obtain more, and not sometimes be content with less?"

Contentment is the Biblical norm. "I have learned," wrote Paul, "in whatsoever state I am, therewith to be content." It's an approach to life that brings happy days and peaceful nights.

Gluttony

In the summer of 1804, as Lewis and Clark's "Corps of Discovery" labored up the Missouri River and penetrated what we now call the Great Plains, the men found themselves in a hunter's paradise. The rich prairie grass supported immense herds of deer, elk, and buffalo, and the streams teemed with fish and beaver.

To young men rowing and poling heavy boats against the Missouri current hour upon hour, and whose rations were hominy, lard, pork, salt pork, flour, and cornmeal, the seemingly endless supply of game was a godsend. Combined with the impure river water they drank, their poor diet had given two-thirds of the men skin ulcers and boils.

But in August, on the plains, things changed for the better. At the end of an exhausting day the men now ate fresh meat: buffalo hump, buffalo tongue, and their favorite, roast beaver tail. They ate a lot, eight to ten pounds a day per man.

Yet these fellows were not gluttons. A nutrition

teacher once told me that adolescent males need as much as four thousand calories a day to provide the fuel for growth and normal teenage activity, and if a boy is in training or in season for athletics, the calorie requirement goes up. Lewis and Clark's young explorers were as lean and tough as boots; their appetites were commensurate with their need.

Not so the glutton. Gluttony, one of the seven deadly sins, is a crime against nature and against the God of creation because it is appetite run amok, consumption with no regard for the body's need or welfare. It is akin to greed and lust in that there is a loss of all proportion. It ignores the intention of the Creator, making means into an end. "Meats for the belly, and the belly for meats," says the glutton, short-circuiting the normal connection between appetite and nutrition.

Gluttonous consumption, in fact, leads away from nutrition to malady. What should be a means of health becomes instead a vehicle of disease, ranging from ailing backs to wrecked cardiovascular systems.

I'm not arguing for a diet of wild rice and alfalfa sprouts. As the statistics on bulimia and anorexia show, obsession with being thin can be every bit as perverse and damaging as overeating. Nor does the

Bible suggest that there's anything wrong with enjoying a good meal. Quite the opposite. Most of the holy days ordered by God for the Israelites included feasting.

Instructions in Deuteronomy 16 for the feast of tabernacles are revealing: "Thou shalt rejoice in thy feast, thou, and thy son, and thy daughter, and thy manservant, and thy maidservant, and the Levite, the stranger, and the fatherless, and the widow that are within thy gates" (verse 14). This feast, coming a week after the grain and grape harvests, was something like our Thanksgiving, but it lasted for a week.

The commands for the tithe of the increase in Deuteronomy 14 indicate that "rejoicing" included hearty eating: oxen, sheep, wine, "whatsoever thy soul desireth...thou shalt eat there before the Lord thy God, and thou shalt rejoice, thou, and thine household" (verse 26).

In translating these events to our culture, we may think of block parties or church picnics, long tables heavy with salads and rolls and fruit and pies, fat sausages, thick burgers, and juicy steaks sizzling and sputtering on big communal barbecues.

And we know that Jesus enjoyed parties with plenty of food. He performed His first miracle, at Cana, so that a wedding feast might not be spoiled. And His carpenter's appetite offended the self-righteous, abstemious Pharisees. "A glutton and a winebibber," they sniffed.

A libel. The Lord of field and flock, of grain and grape, could not abuse the work of His own hands. He ate joyfully and gratefully. Meals need not always be bound by the minimal requirements of human nutrition; they may also be occasions of celebration, fellowship, gratitude, and worship.

Gluttony violates the spirit of Biblical feasting. Since it is habitual, it destroys the sense of occasion of a true feast. Since it is self-centered, it can hardly be in the spirit of fellowship. And since it harms the temple of the Holy Spirit, it clearly cannot be a part of worship.

Feasting is generous; gluttony is selfish. One of the notorious vices of first-century Rome, gluttony infected the church at Corinth, defiling even the Lord's Supper. "In eating every one taketh before other his own supper," Paul said in rebuke. "And one is hungry, and another is drunken."

Jesus, too, was conscious of the hungry. Twice He fed the crowds fish and bread, and on the beach of Galilee He cooked breakfast for hungry fishermen.

We have plenty, most of us. A middle-class American eats better than Louis XIV, who could not expect orange juice in January. It takes many of us just an hour a day to earn enough money to feed our families three meals and a snack.

Just how much food we have was made plain to me by one of my students, a Russian immigrant, who told me of her first trip to an American supermarket. "In Russia I stood in line for three hours outside a store to get a ticket that would allow me to get into the store the next day, just in case the shipment of meat we had heard about might actually come," Sasha said.

"Then, a couple of months after we came to the United States, I took my son Alexei to the store for our first American shopping trip. There was so much! I could not believe the meat counter: beef, chicken, fish, pork—and all different kinds. Pork chops, roast pork, all kind of sausages. Too much. Alexei felt sick to his stomach and had to leave the store. I got a headache. It was overwhelming."

What does all this mean for those who determine to "eat to the Lord"? Jesus' example shows us that our meals are to be occasions of fellowship and worship, marked by gratitude and generosity. Jesus blessed bread and drink, and gave thanks. He gave food to those who had none, and expects us to feed "the least of these my brethren."

Paul's instruction to the Corinthians sums up the issue succinctly: "Whether therefore ye eat, or drink, or whatsoever ye do, do it all to the glory of God" (1 Corinthians 10:31). Words to live by while we wait for the Wedding Feast of the Lamb.

Wrath

After more than forty years of constant, intense, and sometimes frustrating labor, Moses, the great prophet and leader, was denied admission to the Promised Land. To have brought the people out of Egypt, escaped Pharaoh's armies, eaten manna, brought down the commandments from Sinai, followed the pillar of cloud and of fire…to have lived the life of faith, and finally—finally—to *see* the Promised Land but not be allowed in. It must have been a crushingly painful moment for Moses.

And what was this all about, this denial of a holy, forty-year ambition? A righteous man, in a fit of temper, disregarded God's command.

He had good reason for anger. His followers, chronic complainers, were thirsty, and once again blamed Moses and God for their discomfort. They raised loud doubts about God's power and love and about Moses' leadership. Never mind the drowning of a powerful contingent of Egyptian soldiers sent to bring the Israelites back into slavery and infanticide. Never mind the provision of food and sweet water in the desert. Never mind that in a thirsty time Moses struck a rock and God poured out water to slake the thirst of the whole migrating nation. That was in the past. This was now, and no water was in sight.

"Wherefore have ye made us to come up out of Egypt...unto this evil place?" they shouted. "It is no place of [grain] or of figs, or of [grape] vines, or of pomegranates; neither is there any water to drink!" (Numbers 20:5).

God promised once again to give the Israelites what they needed. "Take the rod," He told Moses. "Gather...the assembly together...speak ye unto the rock before their eyes; and it shall [pour] forth his water."

Moses followed God's instructions until the critical moment. And then it was all too much—the complaints, the doubts, the threats. He had had it with these people. "Hear now, ye rebels!" he yelled. And he slammed his rod against the rock once, then again, and a stream gushed out.

No doubt the people were delighted. But God was not. He said to Moses, "Because ye believed me not, to sanctify me...in the eyes of the children of Israel, therefore ye shall not bring this congregation into the land which I have given them." A heavy price to pay for a momentary fit of rage, to be sure.

But prisons are full of men who did not control their tempers and now have years to regret five minutes of murderous anger. I think of a man I'll call Larry. He was a student in a literature class I taught one night a week in a prison. Larry was not a professional criminal; he had been a dairy farmer. Then one night an argument with his wife flamed into violence. A few minutes later she was dead, and Larry had years of shame, grief, remorse, and confinement to face.

He stayed after class one night to talk for a few minutes before he had to go back to his cell. "I saw the parole board today," he said softly. "They told me they didn't even want to talk to me for another ten years. Mr. Hills, my little boy will be a teenager when I get out. He won't know me."

There wasn't much I could say. What had been done could not be undone. Unfettered anger had taken one life and ruined several others, and there were terrible penalties yet to be paid.

We're not very smart when we're angry. The writer of Proverbs observed, "He that is slow to wrath is of great understanding: but he that is hasty of spirit exalteth folly (14:29), and "He that is soon angry dealeth foolishly" (14:17).

When David's men were insulted by Nabal, David was so angry that he decided to kill every man and boy on Nabal's estate. And he would have done it too, if he had not been dissuaded by wise Abigail. When the angry warrior calmed down, he said to Abigail, "Blessed be thy advice, and blessed be thou, [who] hast kept me this day from coming to shed blood."

This story is another reminder of how likely we are to think and behave badly when we're angry, how unlikely we are, with our roused blood roaring in our ears, to be able to hear the voice of reason or sense the prompting of the Holy Spirit. "Let every man be swift to hear, slow to speak, slow to wrath," wrote James, "for the wrath of man worketh not the righteousness of God."

Which of the fruits of the Spirit can we cultivate when we're angry? Love? Joy? Peace? Patience? Gentleness? Goodness? Faith? Do we pray when we're furious? Wrath prompts none of these behaviors. Paul pointed out that wrath keeps company with witchcraft, hatred, strife, jealousy, factions, seditions, heresies, envyings, and murders (Galatians 5:20-21).

Some people seem to be proud of their hot tempers. "It's my Irish blood," they say with a smile and a shrug, as if a bad temper were just a bit of a joke. It's no joke, and prudent people will steer clear of the hothead. "Make no friendship with an angry man," warned Solomon. "With a furious man thou shalt not go: lest thou learn his ways, and get a snare to thy soul" (Proverbs 22:24-25).

A hot temper is no cause of boasting; rather, it should occasion confession and repentance. It is no sign of strength, but rather indicates foolish immaturity. "A fool's wrath is presently known," Solomon said, "but a prudent man covereth shame" (Proverbs 12:16). And later, "Anger resteth in the bosom of fools" (Ecclesiastes 7:9).

Many prisons stipulate anger management training for some inmates hoping for parole. Short of this, how can believers who have volatile tempers bring their emotions more in line with Biblical patterns of forbearance, gentleness, and self-control?

First, we must recognize an evil temper as sin, and confess it, acknowledging that it's ugly, it's harmful, and it violates the commandment to love one's neighbor as oneself.

With this recognition we must determine to pray

for people who provoke us—not so much that their behavior will change to suit us, but for their welfare. We can't be angry at people while we pray for them; it's not possible to accommodate anger and prayer at the same time.

In this vein, when we are irked, we must keep our irritation short rather than nurse it. "Let not the sun go down upon your wrath," is the way the Bible puts it. In short, if we're angry, let's get over it.

Finally, we must cultivate the fruit of the Spirit. This good fruit will crowd out the weeds of wrath and resentment.

Controlling a hot temper is not easy for everyone, but it's a clear expectation for anyone who wants to please the Lord. We must put away our wrath; no one will miss it.

Lust

The philosopher-king sits at his high window, looking out over his capital. It's twilight; the streets are growing cool and quiet, the shops and booths in the bazaar deserted, the seller and the buyer gone home for dinner.

The windows of the stone houses and apartments of Jerusalem fill with the pale yellow-orange light of oil lamps as families recline at low tables laden with cakes of pressed raisins or figs, juicy slices of fresh cucumbers and onions, a plate of roast goat or broiled fish, a stack of pitas.

We may imagine the king satisfied after a busy day as lawmaker, judge and chief executive. The nation's enemies have been subdued, the economy is healthy in spite of high taxes, and the kingdom is at the height of its power.

But in the midst of the peaceful evening the good king spies something disturbing: a youth who "lacks judgment," one of "the simple," headed literally and figuratively in the wrong direction. Instead of making his way home, where his mother sets the table and his father prepares to break the bread, he has ventured the wrong way, down the street to "her" house. This is no innocent, romantic stroll past lilac trees "down the street where you live"; this woman is no bashful maiden. She is "loud and stubborn," she has a brazen face, and there is no mistaking the message of her dress. She's on the make. She's married, but she's not home cooking dinner; she is on the street trolling for men.

Which is, of course, why this foolish young man is headed toward her corner like a homing pigeon, or, as the philosopher puts it, "as a bird hasteth to the snare" (Proverbs 7:23). She is just his kind of woman.

He's headed for trouble, but at the moment he doesn't care. He can't think just now; his circuits are overloaded with long, deep kisses, sexual flattery ("I've been looking for you," she says, "and I've finally found you"), and the prospect of an expensive bedroom fragrant with myrrh, aloes and cinnamon.

And he wants to believe the old lie: "There's no harm done. My husband is out of town on a long business trip. Nobody will ever know."

And the foolish boy heads off to become another notch on her bedpost.

"Dumb as an ox," the wise man observes from his window. "A bird-brain. A fool."

Diagnosis: lust, desire misplaced, mistimed and unregulated by principle or prudence, one of the medieval church's seven deadly sins, deadlier still in the modern age of AIDS.

Let's be clear about this. The problem is not sexual desire, a gift from God celebrated in some of the Bible's richest poetry. The problem is a cancerous form of desire, desire in unseemly multiplication and magnification, desire grown malignant.

Shakespeare, that keen cartographer of the human heart, mapped the terrain of lust in the first ten lines of sonnet 129.

> *Th' expense of spirit in a waste of shame*
> *Is lust in action, and, till action, lust*
> *Is perjured, murd'rous, bloody, full of blame,*
> *Savage, extreme, rude, cruel, not to trust;*
> *Enjoyed no sooner but despise'd straight,*
> *Past reason hunted, and no sooner had,*
> *Past reason hated as a swallowed bait*
> *On purpose laid to make the taker mad:*
> *Mad in pursuit, and in possession so;*
> *Had, having, and in quest to have, extreme...*

The poet could have been commenting on the story of Amnon and Tamar, recorded in 2 Samuel 13. Amnon, obsessed with his half-sister, planned and carried out a rape, in spite of the girl's pleas for decent and proper treatment. "Don't, my brother! Don't force me. Such a thing should not be done in Israel! Don't do this wicked thing... Where could I get rid of my disgrace?"

But Amnon, "mad in pursuit," cared neither for Tamar's future nor for his own. "What about you?" the girl asked. "You would be like one of the wicked fools in Israel."

Lust doesn't listen. Amnon used the girl and, when he was done with her, he "hated her more than he had loved her" (verse 15). "Get this woman out of here," he said to his servant, "and bolt the door after her" (verse 17).

Far different is the abiding passion, generosity, and trust of real love. "I belong to my lover," Solomon's beloved says (7:10), "and his desire is for me... Many waters cannot quench love; rivers cannot wash it away" (8:7)... "I have become in his eyes like one bringing contentment" (8:10).

The inverse of the sin of lust, then, is not the absence of desire. It is the virtue of chastity. The Bible is clear in expressing God's direction on this. For the unmarried the requirement is celibacy; for the married, fidelity.

But chastity, C.S. Lewis observed, is the least popular of the Christian virtues. Our egos, our biology, our culture, even simple loneliness, may all sometimes urge us to betray our best intentions. "The strongest oaths are straw to the fire in the blood," Laertes cautions Ophelia in *Hamlet*, and the toll of judges, politicians and preachers who have blighted their careers with illicit sex confirms Laertes' warning.

Our wise king offers some warnings, too, and with them some advice on how to stay out of trouble. First, in modern vernacular, "If you want to lose weight, don't hang out at the donut shop." The young fool in Proverbs chapter seven put himself in the wrong place to make a good decision. Once he's on her corner the outcome is predictable. "Flee," Paul advised young Timothy. About face and double time. Put some distance between yourself and the temptation.

A second rule: Don't learn to drive from someone who pays a lot for insurance. The young fellow in our story is getting his messages about sex from the wrong place—and as a result he's getting terrible messages: No harm done; nobody will know; it'll be great. The modern parallels are unmistakable. It's hardly surprising that—in a generation getting its messages about love and sex from Hollywood, MTV, and Madison Avenue—nearly one in three babies is born out of wedlock and typically, into poverty, and that the incidence of sexually transmitted diseases has taken on the dimensions of an epidemic.

Instead, says Solomon, "keep your mother's teaching...for these commands are a lamp...the way of life" (Proverbs 6:20, 23).

And while some God-honoring people choose a life of celibate singleness for personal reasons or to better serve the Lord, most of us will marry. For us Solomon has one more rule: keep the home fires burning. "Rejoice with the wife of thy youth," he advises. "Be thou ravished always with her love" (Proverbs 5:18-19).

Always. Because lust is uncommitted and selfish, it's temporary, disappointing and destructive. Chastity, however, refuses to regard other people as occasions for exploitation. Chaste people see sex as part of a whole package of mutual fulfillment and fused identity.

It's easy to tell which approach will find us smiling in the morning.

Sloth

There aren't many jokes in the Bible. Yes, there is ironic humor in the egotistical, Jew-hating Haman having to lead Mordecai, mounted on the emperor's horse, through the streets of ancient Susa bellowing, "Thus shall it be done to the man the king delights to honor."

And there are the funny, sarcastic jibes that Elijah wings at the frantic, sweating prophets of Baal in the showdown at Mount Carmel in 1 Kings 18. "Call louder!" he suggests. Perhaps their god was talking, or deep in thought, or out of town, or taking a snooze.

But the instances of humor, given the size of the Bible, are relatively few. It's of special note, then, to find a figure that is the subject of a number of Biblical jokes. This figure is the sluggard, the lazy oaf. Sometimes this character sounds like the subject of an old comedy shtick: "How lazy is he?" He's so lazy, Proverbs says, that if he gets his hand to the dinner dish he won't even bring it back to his mouth (19:24). To move his hand that far "grieveth him" (26:15).

On the job, this lazybones is like "vinegar to the teeth, and smoke to the eyes" (10:26). But chances are, he won't make it to work anyway; he has creative, if farfetched, excuses for staying in bed, resting on one side and then the other like a door turning upon its hinges (26:14). He can't go to work, he says, because there is a lion in the streets (26:13).

He may not like to work, but he loves to hear himself talk, and his talk is mostly nonsense. "The sluggard is wiser in his own conceit than seven men who can render a reason" Solomon observes (26:16).

For all his conceit, he is dumber than bugs. "Go to the ant," for instruction, Solomon tells him. "Consider her ways and be wise." The ant exemplifies common sense in storing its provisions in summer and gathering its food at harvest (6:6, 8). But rather than working, the lazy man prefers useless get-rich-quick schemes (12:11). He plans, maybe, to win the lottery, or hopes for the chance to sue somebody.

The sluggard is a bozo, all right, and if people shake their heads and laugh at him, it's his own fault. But this is not to say that slothfulness is anything less than a sin. Like all sin, it violates the pattern for life that God gave to Adam, who was put into the Garden of Eden "to dress it and to keep it" (Genesis 2:15).

Slothfulness made the medieval church's list of seven deadly sins. And it is condemned in both the Old and New Testaments.

Why is laziness such a serious sin? To begin with, like all sin, it keeps company with other vices. Contrary to what one might expect, the lazy man, far from being content with a scaled-down standard of living, is often greedy (Proverbs 21:25-26). One thinks of Edwin Arlington Robinson's shiftless Miniver Cheevy. The poet tells us, "Miniver scorned the gold he sought/but sore annoyed was he without it."

Greed wedded to laziness breeds a variety of crimes, from fraud to theft and armed robbery. One reason for the thriving American drug trade is that so much money can be made so fast with such little effort. Besides my work at Corban University, I've taught English courses for the local community college to inmates in several area prisons. One of my students in a federal prison told me calmly, with no trace of boasting, that when he was dealing drugs he made fifty thousand dollars in an average month.

"Fifty thousand?" I said. "Average? What did a really good month look like?"

"Oh," he said, "two hundred, two hundred fifty, around in there."

"Thousand?" I said. "A month?"

"Yeah."

I observed that teaching didn't pay quite that well.

"But look where I am now," he said. "And even before I was arrested I was so ashamed that I gave away all my stuff—my cars, the business and property I bought with dirty money, everything. I'm in prison and I have nothing."

A sad but predictable story. Refuse to work, says Solomon, and want will come "as an armed man" (24:33-34).

American bookshelves and airways swell with advice on how to get rich quick with very little effort: learn how to win at blackjack, get a 900 number and make money every time people call it, think positive. State-sponsored ads urge Oregonians to buy an Oregon lottery ticket and "Adjust your dreams accordingly."

The apostle Paul wrote a very different set of instructions to the Thessalonians. "When we were with you, this we commanded you, that if any would not work, neither should he eat. For we hear that there are some which walk among you disorderly, working not at all, but are busy-bodies. Now them that are such we command and exhort by our Lord Jesus Christ, that with quietness they work, and eat their own bread" (2 Thessalonians 3:10-12).

Industriousness is not to be confused with job obsession. Christians are not to be workaholics. After all, God planned for people to put aside their tools one day a week, rest and worship and give thanks.

But the description of a model wife and mother in Proverbs 31 clearly shows that godly people are to be busy and productive. The good woman enjoys her work (verse 13), puts in a full day (verses 15, 18), is astute in business (verse 16), produces high-quality goods (verse 24) and is efficient (verse 27). She is generous too, sharing her time and profits with the needy (verse 20).

Good work, says the writer of Ecclesiastes, is "from the hand of God" (2:24). It's hardly surprising that he find satisfaction in work; we are created in God's image, and the first thing the Bible tells us about God is that He "created" (Genesis 1:1), "made" (Genesis 1:7), and "worked" (Genesis 2:2-3).

"Whistle while you work," sings a cheerful Snow White. While that advice may be impractical for a judge, an opera star, or a prizefighter, it suggests an approach to the job that finds a parallel in Scripture.

Do all things "heartily, as to the Lord," the apostle Paul wrote (Colossians 3:23).

For Christians, this means that whether we are busy at a desk, on a tractor, or in the pulpit, if we understand that our work is an act of obedience and worship, we are about our Father's business.

Envy

It seems like a small sin. Considering the nightly news reports of the devastation wrought by greed, rage, and lust, envy may strike us as comparatively inconsequential. It seems likely that few of the day's toll of crime victims were robbed, raped, beaten, stabbed, or shot because of envy.

No war crimes tribunal has even been assembled to try, for crimes against humanity, someone accused of mere envy. Nobody has been sent to prison convicted of envy; envy is not illegal.

Yet the medieval church considered envy one of the seven deadly sins, deserving, in its wickedness and toxic effects, to be listed right along with greed, wrath, lust, and their kindred evils that poison the souls of men and work pain and destruction. Envy sets us one against another, man against man, nation against nation. The medieval thinkers and teachers were right in regarding it as a very serious sin indeed.

For one thing, the Bible speaks against envy in clear and strong language. In Galatians chapter five

Paul listed it as one of the acts of the sinful nature. It's an ugly list: "Adultery, fornication, uncleanness, lasciviousness, idolatry, witchcraft, hatred, variance, emulations, wrath, strife, seditions, heresies, *envyings*, murders, drunkenness, revellings, and such like...they which do such things shall not inherit the kingdom of God" (Galatians 5:19-21).

And the great writer Herman Melville pointed out that in its irrationality and spite, envy is "universally felt to be more shameful than even felonious crime." Perhaps the reason for this is it seems so pointless; there is nothing to be gained from it. But as Melville observed, "[Envy's] lodgment is in the heart, not the brain," and is therefore immune from the correction of ordinary decency and common sense.

Envy is a kind of witches' brew of greed, malice, and hate. It violates the two key commandments, "Thou shalt love the Lord thy God with all thy heart, and with all thy soul, and with all thy mind" and "Thou shalt love thy neighbour as thyself" (Mark 12:30-31).

The envious person fails to love God. Instead of love, the envious person harbors a profound ingratitude for God's generous gifts to all and a deep resentment springing from the perception that someone else has a bigger piece of the pie.

And the envious person fails to love his neighbor. "Love does not envy," Paul wrote. Rather than taking pleasure in another's talent or success, the envious man resents the very things that bring others joy.

The results of this sin are devastating. The first person to suffer harm is the one who envies. There is a certain and progressive corrosion of the spirit. "A sound heart is the life of the flesh," the proverb observes, "but envy [is] the rottenness of the bones" (Proverbs 14:30).

The envier grows morose, sullen, bitter. His self-pity and his malicious tongue soon drive away any friends he might once have enjoyed. Envious obsession soon kills any capacity for joy. Envy is a poisonous weed that effectively crowds the fruit of the Spirit out of the garden of the heart, leaving only "things rank and gross in nature." Envy soon metastasizes to more overt and plainly lethal sins. Paul's letter to Titus connected envy with malice and hate (Titus 3:3). From this may come the wish for harm to befall another, and all too often, wishes eventuate in action.

Not for nothing did Jesus equate a hateful heart with murder. It seems likely, for instance, that Cain's murder of his righteous and innocent brother was not the result of a sudden and unforeseen flash of passion, but rather the product of a long spell of brooding, envious resentment and ill will.

Hundreds of years later, the gospels report the same pattern repeated. John recorded that on a day that the leaders of the Jews took up stones to stone Him, Jesus said, "Many good works have I shown you from my Father; for which of those works do ye stone me?"

The answer, apparently, was "For all of them." After all, these people were unhappy when Jesus, outside their auspices, gave sight to the blind. They were furious when, to a man crippled for thirty-eight years, He gave the power to walk. And after He gave life to dead Lazarus, returning him to his loving sisters, the envious leaders set in motion a plot to kill Him.

When they grabbed Jesus in the garden and hustled Him off to Pilate, it didn't take the veteran bureaucrat and judge long to figure out what was going on. "He knew," Matthew wrote, "that for envy they had delivered him" (Matthew 27:18).

A small sin? Hardly. Envy is ugly, deadly, and all too common. I was once struck by the humility, truth, and honesty of a friend who confessed in a prayer, "Lord, none of us is above anything." "Anything" includes envy.

What can we do about it? How best to guard ourselves from this sin? It may at first be one of the quieter sins; its onset may not immediately be apparent—perhaps nothing more than a tic of annoyance at another's success, a failure to rejoice with those who rejoice. But if left to grow, envy has calamitous results. We had better recognize it and deal with it in its early stages.

Care of the soul against the disease of envy begins with prayers. If we are praying for others' welfare, we will be glad in their success and have a sense of sharing in it. That is the outlook the apostle Paul chose, no doubt prayerfully, when some made themselves his rivals in ministry (Philippians 1:12-18). Envy and intercession preclude one another. The prayerful spirit simply has no room for envy.

Nor can envy live with gratitude. The envious man ignores his own gifts from God, dwelling instead on what he perceives to be undeserved blessings granted to another. "Godliness with contentment is great gain," the Scriptures tell us. If we are busy thanking God for His generosity to us, we have little time or inclination to question His generosity to someone else.

Prayer and thanksgiving, then, work together to keep us free of envy, free to enjoy the lives God has given us, and free to multiply our joys by taking genuine pleasure in the joys of others.

Pride

It is the sin, observed C. S. Lewis, that we find most repulsive in others but which we most often tolerate in ourselves. It made the list of seven deadly sins enumerated by the medieval church.

And, though it's doubtful that more than a handful of Baptist and evangelical churches have ever disciplined a member for this sin (we seem to be more sensitive about "sins of the flesh"), it heads the list of things that Proverbs tells us God detests.

Indeed, pride—for this is what we are speaking of—appears to the original sin in heaven, if we understand Ezekiel 28 correctly, and on earth, as indicated in Genesis 3. It is the root from which all other sins rise, the soil from which springs every poisonous weed in the human heart: lies, violence, adultery, theft, greed, fraud, malice, and on the grander scale of things, racism, genocide, and wars of conquest and subjugation.

What was the reason for the estimated 35 million deaths, military and civilian, in World War II, if not pride? In Europe and Asia, far too many people were willing to believe that they were members of a superior race and culture, and they followed the leaders who preached this lie straight to destruction.

It's an old lie—"you will be like gods yourselves." And the consequences are always the same: estrangement from God, estrangement from one another, and bitterness at every hand. And then anything is possible.

For pride justifies every other sin. King Ahab reasoned, *My neighbor's vineyard should be mine, for I am king.* David excused his adultery with the rationalization, *My friend's wife should be mine, for I am king.* Throughout the ages, emperors and common men have justified their sins against others by asserting their superiority.

The gifts of God are never enough for the proud. He believes he is entitled to more. The spouse, the job, the income, the church are never good enough. Even Eden, even heaven, not good enough. "From whence come wars and fightings among you?" James asked. Don't they come from our self-centered desires (James 4:1-4)?

And these desires, the appetites of the ungoverned ego, regard other people as means or as obstacles, to be used or to be overcome. People are loved for what advantage or service they can provide, which means, of course, they are loved not at all.

The conduct of the Pharisees demonstrates this point: they prayed, they tithed, they went often to the temple, but their righteous-looking behavior was less in the service of God than in the service of self. They did all this, said Jesus, to be seen of men. And they got what they wanted. But they despised the very people for whose acclaim they lusted. They cared nothing for the penitent sinner; Pharisees need the publican to stay sinful so they can congratulate themselves on their own righteousness.

Nor were they pleased when a man took his first step in thirty-eight years (John 5). It seems that the healing had occurred outside the Pharisees' jurisdiction, and this, not the health of the healed man, was what mattered.

The Biblical treatment prescribed for the sin of pride is not self-contempt or self-effacement. The quiet and shy may, in fact, be every bit as proud as the talkative and outgoing. Pride is not a matter of personality; it is the central sin of the human spirit, and it must be treated as every other sin we recognize in ourselves. We must learn to hate it as God hates it, to confess it, repent of it, to seek by the power of the Word and the Holy Spirit to root it out of our lives, and to grow the grace of humility in its place.

Humility is perhaps the least understood of the Biblical virtues. Humility is not the same as humiliation, spiritlessness, or an avoidance of responsibility. It is the devotion to a cause greater than one's own ego.

Humility requires us to assess our own abilities accurately and to devote those abilities to the service of God and others (Philippians 2:1-8). The best scorer on a basketball team may properly want the ball in the closing moments of a tight game. The most talented singer should sing. In the parable of the talents, Jesus made it clear that our Master has given each of us special abilities in trust. He also made it clear that God expects us to exercise these abilities and holds us accountable for what we do with what He has given us.

And perhaps genuine humility lies right here, in the recognition that nothing we have—not money, nor intelligence, nor a quick, strong body, nor a beautiful voice or face, nor our children, nor our very selves—is our own. All of these and more are gifts to be gratefully returned to God in ways that bring Him glory (Colossians 3:23).

Submission seems to be the key to humility. "Submit yourselves to God," commanded James. "Submit to one another out of reverence for Christ," counseled Paul. This does not mean that the soloist with the beautiful voice should defer to someone who sounds like a crow with a cold. It means that the canary and the crow give thanks to God for the song and worship Him together, with each doing what he does humbly to the glory of God.

When a father submits to the requirements of his office—the welfare of his children—he understands that his son's Little League team exists for the enjoyment of the child, not the ego of the father, and that it is not the son's obligation to somehow make the father look good by turning every at-bat into a line drive or every game into a win.

Pride separates and alienates people, as it alienated the first humans from one another, from their environment, and from God. Few churches split over doctrinal issues. More commonly the rift grows out of what are politely called "personality clashes," collisions of egos and wills. Pride. Imagine the absurdity, said Paul, of a proud eye saying to the hand, "I don't need you." When the eye and hand and head and feet fail to work together we have a body that is diseased and crippled (1 Corinthians 12).

Submission is not degrading; it is fulfilling, yielding to a sovereign Lord to serve and glorify Him in any way that can please Him.

Let the people of God build, sing, teach, write, exhort, paint, cook, compose, run, grow flowers, lay brick, visit the sick, encourage the weak, all to the glory of the Redeemer. For when we turn our attention to glorifying Him, we embrace true humility and repentance and come home to our Father's house.

The Classic Christian Virtues

Patience

Patience is a quiet virtue. No medal is stamped to recognize it; no mayor or president makes a speech honoring its practice. Like housecleaning, it is more noticeable "in the breach than in the observance."

Nevertheless, patience is a foundational element in the Christian character, a mark of emotional and spiritual maturity and a central trait of the life of faith.

The young, who seem to have plenty of time before them, are impatient. "How much farther?" children in the car ask again and again. "Are we almost there?" "When will it be Christmas?" Later, in adolescence, they have large appetites, and it's hard for them to wait. They like fast food, fast cars, quick results.

But the young aren't the only ones who struggle. Impatience, the expectation of instant gratification, is part of the very wiring of an electronic society that promises "fast, fast, fast" pain relief, rapid weight loss, instant success (just phone in your credit card number for the $79.95 video telling how to program yourself to succeed), and quick and easy money.

"It's easy," the telegenic young man insists. "I'll show you how to get people to call your special 900 number. You'll make money with every call—even when you're asleep."

Here in Salem, the busy capital of Oregon, one law firm, whose offices, once a bank, front a bustling downtown street, kept a drive-through window. For those impatient to end a marriage the sign read, "Drive-Through Divorce."

The Bible offers a different view, linking patience with wisdom and faith. Far from offering a formula for fast pain relief, James reminds us that the follower of Jesus must learn to regard painful circumstances as opportunities for growth.

Just as hard, consistent athletic training produces physical toughness and endurance, difficult trials in the believer's life are necessary for the maturation of Christian character.

"The trying of your faith produces patience," James counseled. "And let patience have her work, so that you may be perfect (mature), lacking nothing." This is the road to wisdom. "If any of you lack wisdom let him ask of God, who giveth to all men liberally."

Patience here means perseverance, a willingness

to accept the sometimes uncomfortable process of maturation. In the midst of painful circumstances the impatient and immature person cries, "Why? Why is this happening to me? I want to get out of this!" The patient person asks, "What? What can I learn from this? I want to be wiser."

The impatient person learns nothing from his trials. He asks for wisdom on his own terms, not God's. He is like the student who comes to my office to ask how to do better in the course he is taking from me, and then refuses to submit to the hours of disciplined study that success requires. He wants a formula for quick and easy success, and there is none.

Patience understands that the road to wisdom is long and sometimes painful. There are no shortcuts or easy rides. It understands, too, that the wise person accepts God's processes and God's timing.

We speak of "the patience of Job." But Job's patience was actually the refusal to accept any quick, defective formula to account for his suffering, or to end that suffering by his own means.

"Curse God and die," Job's bitter wife urged. Very simple, and utterly wrong. In his patience and wisdom, Job took a wider view: "Shall we accept good from God but not trouble?"

His friends offered yet another formula: "There is a direct correlation between specific sin and specific suffering. You must have done something pretty bad to deserve this kind of punishment. You'd better admit it. Confess your sin, and your suffering will end."

There is a kind of moral mathematics in such a line of reasoning that is appealing in its tidiness and simplicity. It is also wrong.

Applying the same flawed formula, Jesus' disciples asked about the man born blind: "Who did sin, this man, or his parents?" (John 9:2). Jesus replied, "Neither hath this man sinned, nor his parents: but that the works of God should be made manifest in him."

The wisdom of patience, then, does not demand simple answers, but in times of trouble and perplexity remains confident in God's love and power. Amid a storm of sorrow, pain, and false accusations, Job, battered and stunned, still insisted, "I know that my Redeemer liveth, and that he shall stand at the latter day upon the earth."

Patience looks past the now to the end. It has faith, not only in God's purposes, but also in His timing. Must we march around Jericho for a whole week? Very well, a week it shall be.

This is the patience of David, who, though anointed king years earlier, refused to kill the reigning king, Saul, even to defend himself. When David had the chance to ambush Saul, end Saul's threat to himself, and become king, his young warriors urged him to do it. But David declared, "The Lord forbid that I should do this thing unto my master, the Lord's anointed." He trusted God's purpose and God's timetable. He could wait.

It is the patient humility of Paul, who recognized that the outcome and timing of ministry are in the hands of God, and that visible results may not be immediate: "I have planted, Apollos watered; but God gave the increase" (1 Corinthians 3:6).

And the ability to look past the now toward God's promised outcome is the patience of all those who "wait for His appearing."

"How long?" we may ask as the morning paper and the evening news recite the daily menu of catastrophe and evil: children cooking their brains with vicious drugs, Little-League-aged boys ambushing classmates with rifle fire, girls in their mid-teens dumping their newborn babies into trash bins, terrorists bombing busy markets. In the "patience of hope" we wait "for that which we see not," confident that in due time all will be put right. Until then, Jesus says to those of "an honest and good heart, having heard the word, *keep it, and bring forth fruit with patience*" (Luke 8:15).

Self-Control

"Let it all hang out," urged the flag-bearers of the social revolution of the sixties. "If it feels good, do it."

Whatever was "natural" was deemed good. To say no to a human impulse was to thwart the exercise of healthy freedoms, resulting in emotional, social, and political repression. Self-control? In that direction lurked neuroses and totalitarianism.

The Bible says something different. Scripture lists self-control as a fruit of the Spirit, and the church has long included self-control as one of the classic Christian virtues.

The reasons for this are plain. Scripture and human experience tell us that not all "natural" impulses are healthy, and that following them, not resisting them, may lead to madness and totalitarianism.

Human nature frequently manifests itself in ways that are anything but benign. As the apostle Paul said, the sinful nature desires what is contrary to the Spirit. Its behaviors are obvious: adultery, fornication, impurity and debauchery; idolatry, witchcraft, hatred, jealousy, fits of rage, selfish ambition, dissension, factionalism, envy, drunkenness, orgies, and such like. That list, taken from Galatians 5:19-21, is not pretty. And human beings who refuse to discipline themselves are not pretty, either.

Self-control is a fundamental trait of maturity. Without it, people remain whining adolescents who regard their own desires as the central interest of the universe.

For a dozen years or more I taught writing and literature courses to inmates in three area prisons. I enjoyed the work and found many of my inmate students to be bright and articulate. I respected their interest in gaining an education and entertained hope that their foolish, dangerous, and arrogant behavior might change.

And some did change. The baddest of the bad, Big Mike, large, mean and dangerous, gave himself to the Lord.

I had learned to be cautious over jailhouse conversions, but Mike didn't play games. His demeanor changed, his countenance changed, and his reputation began to change.

But too many of his fellow inmates continued in

the same attitudes that had repeatedly led them into trouble. They were, in many respects, still thinking and behaving like children, spectacularly self-centered and amazingly impulsive. And even in prison, rather than learning to control their lawless desires, they too often schemed to indulge them.

They strutted, they bragged, they carried on a drug trade, they conned foolish women into sending them money. And they watched hour upon hour of television cartoons.

"When I was a child, I spake as a child, I understood as a child," Paul wrote to the Corinthian believers. "But when I became a man, I put away childish things."

Children know nothing of appropriate speech. They simply blurt out whatever crosses their mind. They are prisoners of the immediate. They know nothing of saying no to appetite because they can't tell where their urges might take them.

Grown-ups take a longer view: too much candy brings on stomach aches. It's better to say no now than to have to deal with the consequences of foolish self-indulgence.

Self-control is an exercise in considering consequences, in escaping the tyranny of the present.

King David, that passionate man, too often acted on impulse.

Insulted by the surly Nabal, David ordered his fighting men to saddle up. They were going to kill every man and boy on Nabal's estate. Fortunately this band of fire-eyed raiders was intercepted by a wise and prudent woman.

"Let no evil or wrongdoing be found in you," Abigail advised David. "When the Lord shall have done for you all the good that He has promised and has appointed you ruler over Israel, you will not have the grief of remembering that you shed blood without just cause." First Samuel 25 records the full story.

Abigail was thinking ahead. And David listened to her mature counsel, saying no to his own impulse to exact revenge for an insult, an impulse entirely human, and entirely wrong.

Perhaps it helped that the intercessor was a woman. An appreciation of feminine grace and beauty was part of David's character too. There's nothing wrong with that, but, unchecked and ungoverned, this led to later trouble. David's failure to govern his own sexual desires eventuated in adultery and murder, and his authority as a father and a king was forever compromised.

The story of David and Bathsheba tells us all we need to know about the consequences of a loss of self-control. But we don't need to confine our thinking to capital crimes to be reminded of the serious and permanent results of neglecting this virtue. James addressed the necessity of controlling our tongues.

If there is anyone who is never at fault in what he says, James wrote such a person is "a perfect man, able also to bridle the whole body," or keep himself in check.

And if we fail to control our speech? "Behold, how great a matter a little fire kindleth! And the tongue is a fire...an unruly evil." Another writer put it this way: "He that keepeth his mouth keepeth his life: but he that openeth wide his lips [speaks rashly] shall have destruction" (Proverbs 13:3).

Let it all hang out? Human experience, common sense, and the Bible say otherwise. To the glutton the Lord says, "Put a knife to your throat" (Proverbs 23:2). To the impulsive young, "[Get] wisdom, and instruction and understanding" (Proverbs 23:23). To those who would rather linger in bed than go to work: "Go to the ant...consider her ways, and be wise... How long wilt thou sleep?"

We all have impulses that must be controlled.

Sometimes we need to stand when we feel like running, keep quiet when we want to blurt out some ill-advised remark, calm down when we feel ourselves growing angry.

Self-control isn't always easy, but it is a divine expectation. And through prayer, discipline, and the work of the Holy Spirit, it is a virtue within reach of every one of us.

Love

Renée looked into her bridegroom's eyes. "I will," she pledged.

Her voice was firm and clear, not surprising to those of us who had seen her perform in college productions. But she had never been quite this graceful, poised, and beautiful.

She will be a good wife, I thought. *Smart, industrious, articulate, gentle. That young man will bless this day for a long time to come.*

"I will." With those words Renée had promised to love her bridegroom until parted by death.

It was, I suppose, an easy thing to say at the moment, this culmination of months of courtship enhanced by music, candlelight, and the perfect dress. Still, I knew Renée would not make such a promise casually under any circumstances. This marriage would last and prosper.

But what of the fifty of every hundred other couples repeating wedding vows today who would someday regret it? Why would half of today's marriages disintegrate? Weren't those couples equally serious when they made their vows?

I'm sure they were. And I'm sure there are many reasons why so many happy and well-intentioned brides and grooms eventually find themselves unable or unwilling to continue in a marriage begun with such high hopes and heartfelt promises. One reason, I suspect, is that they were not clear about what they were saying when they promised to love one another until parted by death.

Did they think they meant that they would always feel the way they felt at the altar? Did they imagine that their entire married life would be an extended honeymoon, that their heartbeats would be perpetually fueled by what John Updike has called "the mad chemistry" of Eros?

If that's what they thought, they were certain to be disillusioned, for this sort of passion is not perpetual. Passion helps bring men and women together, and it is part of a good marriage. But by itself, passion cannot sustain us.

It is no great insight to observe than that popular culture has made erotic love a commodity. Through film and song people of our time are trained to perceive "love" as a collection of self-conscious gestures and sensations. That concept is wildly inadequate as a basis for enduring relationships, since once the other person no longer makes us feel "seven stories high," that person's usefulness to us is ended.

A more mature, Biblically-based understanding of love has less to do with how we feel than with what we value. Our values direct our behaviors.

When I made my own wedding vows, I announced that "from this day forward" I would regard nothing as strictly my own, neither my possessions, nor my time, nor even my own body. I had no more exclusive claims on anything. I gave it all to the woman on whose hand I slipped a gold ring.

I pledged that from now on, her welfare was to be my chief concern. And I would not count myself exempt on days when she misplaced the car keys, or drank the last Coke in the fridge, or talked when I wished her to listen. Or even when she was irritable and, in my view, unreasonable.

I had promised to behave in certain ways, to adopt attitudes and to engage in actions that made her worth and welfare my highest priorities. I had *not* promised to "feel" a certain way. Nobody can, in good conscience, promise to feel any certain way a week, or a month, or a year from now.

When the Lord commands me to love my neighbor as myself, He is not ordering me to try to manufacture an emotion; He is requiring me to act in a loving way—to give my neighbor the benefit of the doubt, to give him a coat if he needs one, to be easily entreated, to overlook his faults, to forgive his real or imagined offenses, to pray for him. To treat my neighbor, in short, the way I like to be treated.

The greatest of the commandments, to "love the Lord thy God," also is defined in terms that go beyond questions of mood or emotional elevation. Certainly, making "a joyful noise" is part of our expression of love and appreciation of God's character and ways. But eventually even the most enthusiastic singers have to pause for breath. Then what?

Jesus gave us the answer. It's direct, succinct, and in the imperative. If you love Me, He said, keep My commandments. James insisted, in his epistle, that the test of faith is action. Jesus said that the same test of action applies to love.

The love of God Himself is evidenced and expressed in action. It's defined, in John 3:16, by a verb: "God so loved the world that he gave..." And when the Lord talked about what it means to love one's neighbor, He told a story about a Samaritan who *did* things, things that were inconvenient and expensive.

Love costs. It's not an investment in the sense that we calculate the returns. If we love our children, we do not keep records of the money we spent on their food, their shoes, their education, their medical expenses, and then, when they reach maturity, present them with a bill. No, we simply find joy in contributing to their welfare. Our concern has been with them, not with ourselves.

But the paradox of love is that this sort of self-forgetfulness and apparent self-diminishment is the way of growth. A man absorbed in himself is a man confined in a small place. Romeo was right when he exclaimed that his love enabled him to "o'er perch these walls," those "stony limits" of the Capulet estate. Love is the way beyond all our stonyhearted limits.

And love is a choice. When Jesus commanded us to love our enemies, He did not ask us to pretend that they were pleasant people. He simply ordered us to act in a loving way, to pray for them.

And prayer, which is a generosity of spirit, combined with generosity of deed, will ensure that we *feel* the right way too.

Gratitude

September 4, 1999

How is it that the most prosperous decade in American history—probably in human history—has come to be called the Whiny Nineties? A recent *Newsweek* cover identifies "The Whine of '99: 'Everyone's getting rich but me.'"

"Call our era the Age of Entitlement," writes Robert J. Samuelson. Following WWII "we had a grand vision... We expected all social problems to be solved...most workers would have rising incomes... We expected almost limitless personal freedom and self-fulfillment. We not only expected these things. After a while, we thought we were entitled to them as a matter of right."

Chuck Colson described these social phenomena as a "blight of discontent." This blight begins with ingratitude, a failure to regard the blessing of life as the gifts that they are, and a sense that these gifts are in fact less than we deserve.

The ingrate always believes he deserves more.

Supply will never catch up with his demand, and the gap between them is his field of discontent.

One of the lessons from Job is that nothing we have is ours. We are not entitled to anything. Job understood this. "The Lord giveth and the Lord taketh away," he said in a time of great loss. "Blessed be the name of the Lord."

His wife had no such understanding. The Lord took away the things she believed were hers by right: her family's wealth, her family itself, her husband's health. As these gifts vanished one by one she was not inclined to bless the name of the Lord. "Curse God and die," she advised her stricken husband.

Ingrates are bitter. Neither their neighbors nor their boss nor God, they believe, have accurately calculated their worth.

Ingratitude partakes of pride and of greed. The promotion and raise at work, the award of recognition in the community, the "good and perfect gifts" from heaven are never enough. So the ingrate is sullen and unhappy. And because his sense of entitlement is open-ended he always will be sullen and unhappy.

Gratitude is one of the classic Christian virtues. The grateful person recognizes the gifts of God and takes joy in them. Every meal is cause for celebration, every grape on the tongue a reminder of how the Creator and Sustainer of the universe has spun rain and earth and wood into deliciousness. Every bite of fragrant, crusty bread speaks of the Bread of Life and the good hungers that He satisfies.

Ingratitude is the certain road to discontent, and the kind of murmuring and complaining that tries God's patience.

In the Exodus from slavery and genocide to freedom and prosperity the ungrateful Hebrews found the oases too far apart, the diet too bland. Rather than offering daily prayers of gratitude for God's guidance, deliverance and provision, they complained that they missed the melons and cucumbers of Egypt. "Our souls loathe this light bread," they grumbled as God gave them manna every morning.

In Egypt their baby boys had been thrown to the crocodiles, and now, in the presence of their living sons, they complained about their breakfast. This sort of moral blindness is typical of ingrates.

Gratitude recognizes God's hand in His creation and in the affairs of men, and is moved to acknowledge that He doeth all things well. This is no less true in difficult circumstances. "Count it all joy," said James, "when you encounter various trials."

The reason? Gratitude for God's training program. Athletes know that a demanding preseason training regimen is a good thing, and that a coach who makes them work harder than they want to actually is doing them a favor.

On a recent late-summer night I watched a college volleyball game in a too-warm gym. The home team struggled to win the first game. The second they won handily, and early in the third game the visitors folded. It was easy to see which coach had put her players through a tough fitness program.

"It's a good feeling to know we're in the best condition," one of the players, sweat-soaked and smiling, told me after the match. She wasn't even breathing hard.

Gratitude is a habit of character. "In everything give thanks," the apostle wrote. "Count your blessings," the old gospel song advises.

It's easy to fault the nine lepers Jesus healed for neglecting to thank the Great Physician. But perhaps we too neglect to thank Him for giving us clean limbs, for giving us sight, for presenting to us, as He did to Jairus and the widow of Nain, our daughters and sons.

On the first Saturday one September I stood outside the doors of a sunlit chapel and watched my two sons, one on each side of their mother, tuck her hands into the crooks of their strong arms, and escort her down the aisle to take her place as the mother of the bride.

The late afternoon sun set the stained glass windows aglow. On the first step of the platform a broad-shouldered, handsome young man gazed toward the rear of the chapel, smiling. The string quartet paused. A trumpeter played the first notes of "Trumpet Voluntary."

My daughter gripped my hand—hard.

"Are you ready, Baby?" I asked quietly.

She nodded. Her eyes were shiny.

"All right, then. Here we go."

"I love you, Daddy."

"I know; I love you, too," I said, and we stepped through the double doors and walked together into the music and the gold and crimson light.

Light was shed, too, on the times when being a parent had been difficult: trying to soothe a colicky baby in the small hours, the hours and the money—a lot of both—invested in developing her athletic talent, extra work to help pay tuition and buy expensive textbooks. Now, from this perspective, I was grateful for it all.

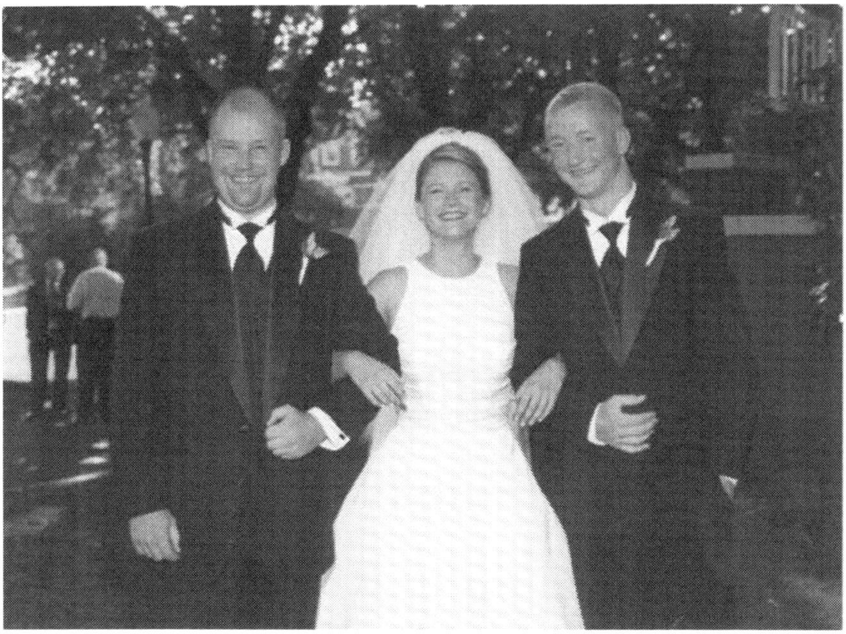

Compassion

"We are trying to help young criminals see their victims and the victims' families as real," James Anderson is telling me over enchiladas about his work with what are politely called "juvenile offenders." These kids are in their early- to mid-teens, boys and girls one might expect to be playing junior varsity baseball or doing homework.

But while others their age take batting practice or study algebra, these youngsters are doing time. They are locked up, and with good reason. Some of them are local, and I remember when a couple of them made the headlines: the kid whose street name was Carnage shotgunning two boys to death outside a popular sandwich shop, and the clean-cut boy who ambushed his mother on a walking path and stabbed her twenty-two times.

Most of the dangerous youngsters James has worked with the last dozen years have had less press, but their conversations about their crimes have a chilling consistency, descriptions of an outlook on life and a frame of mind at the time of the crime that fail to regard the victims as real people, human beings who feel fear and pain and loss. "The antithesis of compassion isn't hatred," James observed. "It's detachment."

Thousands of people complicit in the extermination of millions of European Jews in the early 1940s denied any particular animosity toward the people they helped along the way to the gas chambers and the great ovens, a denial that is all too plausible. Mechanics, engineers, bricklayers, stationmasters, pipefitters—they were just doing their job, just following orders, they said.

Perhaps so. But at some level of consciousness this complicity required the perpetrators to regard the victims as other than themselves. The yellow Star of David required to be worn on the coat of "der Jude" marked him as alien, an other, not a neighbor to be regarded and loved as oneself. He could be viewed with detachment, and eventually he was disposable, like a wad of waste paper or an old tire. Those who, day after day, herded human beings on and off the cattle cars and sorted them out, the old or small or weak straight to the gas, the others to a level of deprivation and labor that would in time be as lethal as cyanide, didn't need to hate them, they only needed to have ceased to regard them, to have come to view Samuel or Rachel or little Lev as something like a lump of coal in a carload of coal.

Compassion—fellow feeling—one of the classic Christian virtues, begins with seeing. As the prodigal son limped home, destitute and dirty, "when he was yet a great way off, his father saw him, and had compassion, and ran, and fell on his neck, and kissed him." The father could see past the filthy clothes and the matted hair. He saw a real person: "my son," he said, "alive again."

And at the pool of Bethesda, John reports, among the "great multitude" of "blind, halt, withered," there lay a man who had been crippled for thirty-eight years. Many in Jerusalem walked past him every day. Some left him a few coins. But his healing encounter with Jesus began "when Jesus saw him."

To most passersby the crippled man had simply blended into the scene, like one of the pillars. Some cared so little about him that they were unhappy that he had been healed on the Sabbath—the wrong day, in their opinion, to get well and carry your mat from the place of begging.

They could not have been thinking about him, a

real person who wanted to walk. They had words for him—cripple, beggar, sinner—that simply filed him away, practically out of sight.

Not so Jesus. "When he saw the multitudes," Matthew wrote, "he was moved with compassion on them, because they fainted, and were scattered abroad, as sheep having no shepherd."

Loving one's neighbor begins with seeing him and in some sense being him in one's imagination. When Jesus saw the cripple he experienced something of life lived on the unforgiving stone of the pavement, the frustration of missed opportunity at the waters that were said to heal, the daily humiliation of surviving on the casual coins of those more powerful and more wealthy.

And isn't this the essence of the incarnation, of God become man? Our Creator became one of us. He lived for a while as one of us. He knew hunger and thirst, and the flavor of broiled fish and bread, and the feel of cool water on a dry throat. He enjoyed weddings and he held children in his arms. He was tested in every way that we are. He knew how it felt to be betrayed by someone close to Him. He was, Isaiah said, "acquainted with grief." He knows our frame. He identifies with us.

Not so the Pharisee. "I thank God," he prays, "that I am not like other men." This self-proclaimed detachment from the sorrows and the joys of other humans goes a long way toward explaining why the Pharisee takes no pleasure in the repentance of the sinner or the healing of the cripple. He feels no connection with them. They are other.

The prophet Jonah had the same moral arrogance and lack of imagination. He felt no connection with the alien Ninevites, though it can't be said that he was merely indifferent to their fate. No, he would have been all too happy to observe their destruction. The self-righteous are good haters. "I knew that thou art a gracious God, and merciful, slow to anger, and of great kindness," he complained in a ridiculous indictment of God's character. This from a man who cared more about a gourd than about the children of the great city of Nineveh, hardly evidence of moral acuity.

"The Lord is gracious and full of compassion," the Psalmist wrote (145:8). If we are to have His mind we must be the same. We must see what others see, feel what others feel, and extend to others the grace and forgiveness that we ourselves have received.

Faith

For a long time I thought faith mostly meant trying to believe improbable things, a kind of mental gymnastics apparently possible for a few highly trained intellectual contortionists, but not for me.

"Only believe," a popular preacher-healer insisted, and all things would be possible. Did you suffer from tinnitus, arthritis or cancer? Simply believe in the power of divine healing and, when he put his hand on you, you would be cured. The corollary attached to this axiom was simple, too: if you were still sick you obviously did not have enough faith.

The implications of this were cruel. If the healing attempt failed, you were worse off than before. Now you were responsible for your illness, a sinner as well as a patient. Your faith was inadequate. It and you had been tested and found wanting.

Dismissing the claims of the tent-show evangelists was easy. Their program was, after all, the perfect setup. How hard could it be to make believers of people who so desperately wanted to believe, especially with the built-in understanding that the failure to be the recipient of a miracle was due to one's own defect of faith? This kind of faith must be for the painfully and irresponsibly credulous.

Still, the recognition of misplaced faith and false faith, and the abuse and exploitation they invite, didn't help define genuine faith. Nor did it negate scriptural admonitions on the virtue of faith: "Without faith it is impossible to please Him" (Hebrews 11:6) and "if you have faith and doubt not...you can say to this mountain, 'Go throw yourself into the sea,' and it will be done. If you believe, you will receive whatever you ask for in prayer" (Matthew 21:21).

Obviously Jesus, as he frequently did, was employing metaphor and hyperbole to make a point. But what point? What could he mean by such a statement?

First, he did not mean that faith is whimsical. God is not a genie to be summoned whenever we want a favor. James points out that prayers generated from selfish motives are misdirected and futile. The genuine prayer of faith is an exercise in submission to God.

Put another way, faith is not linked to a particular outcome. James and Peter were both arrested by Herod. Peter was granted a miraculous delivery from prison and execution; James had his head cut off. Did Peter have more faith than James? The Bible offers no suggestion that he did—or even that Peter and his friends were praying for Peter's *deliverance.* They may have been praying not for escape, but for courage and faithfulness for one who, in a previous crisis, had denied his Lord.

This time Peter does not panic. Rather, he goes to sleep, confident that God is working and content that His will be done. Peter the Rock is not anxious over the immediate event.

Nor were the three Hebrew friends in the book of Daniel. They did not know, when they refused to grovel before the emperor's colossal image, that God would protect them from Nebuchadnezzar's rage and fire. "Bow," said the tyrant. "Do it now." Otherwise, "Ye shall be cast the same hour into the midst of a burning fiery furnace; and who is that God that shall deliver you out of my hands?"

But there was no use threatening these men. While not privy to God's plans, they were determined to obey Him. Immediate outcomes were not their concern. "O Nebuchadnezzar," they replied, "we are not careful to answer thee in this matter. If it be so, our God whom we serve is able to deliver us from the burning fiery furnace, and he will deliver us out of thine hand, O king. But if not...we will not serve thy gods, nor worship the golden image which thou hast set up" (Daniel 3:16-18).

They refused to renege on what they knew to be true. Not so the faithless Israelites in the exodus. Again and again God had demonstrated His power and His loving intentions. He had prepared and sent a prophet to lead them from slavery to independence. He had forced an emperor to give up his free labor; He had parted the waters, drowned the Egyptian soldiers, provided a pillar of fire and a pillar of cloud to guide the nation through the wilderness. There was no doubt about who was in control.

But at Sinai, when Moses did not return from the mountain as soon as the people thought he should, they turned their backs on the truth, ignoring all the things Jehovah had done for them.

Instead, they manufactured another explanation. They created an idol, a golden calf, and declared, "These be thy gods, O Israel, that brought you out of Egypt."

Surely they knew better. But under the pressure of the moment they chose to ignore the history of God's wisdom, love and provision.

Memory is crucial to faith. God does not ask for belief in a vacuum. Biblical narratives have been preserved for us as a record of God's faithfulness over the centuries. And Biblical prophecies record an outline of His plan for the future. We need to know the stories, and we need to know what they mean.

Put another way, "faith comes by hearing." Genuine faith is not, as some would have it, a crutch for the ignorant; it is the spiritual vehicle of the Biblically literate. Without knowing the sacred stories, we have no way of understanding God's dealings with His people, and no basis for confidence in Him.

When the Israelites finally emerged from the wilderness they were confronted with one final barrier to their promised land: the Jordan River in flood. The story of their crossing is astonishing: "As soon as the priests who carried the ark reached the Jordan and their feet touched the water's edge, the water from upstream stopped flowing" (Joshua 3:15-16).

The people crossed the riverbed, and before the river's flow was restored, God ordered that a man from each of the twelve tribes retrieve a rock from the bottom of the river to build a monument, so that "in the future, when your children ask you, 'What do these stones mean,' tell them that the flow of the

Jordan was cut off before the ark of the covenant of the Lord" (4:6-7).

The faith of the next generation was not to be a matter of temperament or passing mood or religious manipulation; it was to be a matter of record.

If we expect our children to be faithful in the future we had better be faithful to the past. Our worship must be built on the knowledge of what God has done. Only then can we have confident faith in what He will do.

Humility

Of the classic Christian virtues humility may be the least understood. It is sometimes mistakenly equated with timidity, shyness, or self-deprecation.

But it is none of these. Moses was not being humble in the biblical sense when he resisted God's commission. "I will send thee unto Pharaoh," the Lord said from the burning bush, "that thou mayest bring forth my people the children of Israel out of Egypt."

But Moses, Egyptian prince in exile and now mere shepherd, doesn't want the job. "Who am I, that I should go unto Pharaoh, and that I should bring forth the children of Israel out of Egypt?" he protests. "They will not believe me... I am not eloquent...but I am slow of speech and of a slow tongue" (Exodus 3, 4).

It's clear that God did not regard Moses' reluctance as stemming from genuine humility. Indeed, "the anger of the Lord was kindled against Moses" (Exodus 4:14).

After all, Jehovah had been preparing Moses for this great task from the moment of his birth in Egypt at a time when Hebrew boys were born under a death sentence. In an astonishing turn of events the Lord had preserved baby Moses, moved him into the Egyptian royal household, provided him with years of the best education in the world, and then brought him to Midian to learn how to live in the desert.

It was time for the people of Israel to be delivered from Egypt, cross the wilderness and make new homes in Canaan.

For this great enterprise they needed a great leader. If not Moses, then who? Who else had his training? Who else had his commission? God promised, "Certainly I will be with thee," and "they shall hearken to thy voice," and "I will be with thy mouth, and teach thee what thou shalt say." False humility was not called for; confident obedience was.

Humility is not the opposite of godly confidence; it is the opposite of self-aggrandizement. Genuinely humble Christians understand that they have been given talents, gifts and training to be used in the service of others. Paul never introduced himself as Paul the scholar or Paul the writer, but as "a servant of Jesus Christ, called to be an apostle."

"Let nothing be done through strife or vain glory," he wrote the Christians in Philippi, "but in lowliness of mind let each esteem others better than themselves."

"Self-esteem" has become a tiresome buzzword in modern education. We're told that children can't learn unless they first have self-esteem, and it's no doubt true that cowed, humiliated and abused kids have a hard time learning. But it hardly follows that healthy youngsters need an infusion of self-esteem (whatever that means) before they can buckle down to study. Indeed, learning at its best is an act of self-forgetfulness. The lab experiment, the poem and the history lesson are interesting and valuable in their own right, not merely for how they may relate to the student.

God has granted us in creation all the dignity we need. Godly humility recognizes, with the psalmist, that human beings are "crowned with glory and honor," rulers "over the works of [God's] hands...flocks and herds, and the beasts of the field, the birds of the air, and the fish of the sea" (Psalm 8).

There is no need, then, for us to be vigilant in defending the borders of our psyches. The biblically humble person is a free person, free from the cynical calculus of ego enhancement, free from the shabby gray walls of defensiveness, free to enjoy and celebrate the gifts and accomplishments of others created in God's image, and free to serve.

Humility, like love, does not keep score, but finds joy in service itself. Jesus said of the arrogant and self-righteous Pharisees, "all their works they do for to be seen of men… [T]hey love…greetings in the markets, and to be called of men, Rabbi, Rabbi. But be not ye called Rabbi: for one is your master, even Christ; and all ye are brethren…and whosoever shall exalt himself shall be abased; and he that shall humble himself shall be exalted" (Matthew 23).

This humility is not, to be sure, the way to win a presidential election; it is the way to live a loving and joyful life honoring to the Lord and to one another. For the biblically humble, service is an ordinary disposition. They do what should be done without thinking much about it and without keeping track.

But God keeps track. One day, said Jesus, the king will say to the quietly righteous, "Come, ye blessed of my Father, inherit the kingdom prepared for you…for I was an hungered, and ye gave me meat: I was thirsty and ye gave me drink: I was a stranger, and ye took me in: naked, and ye clothed me: I was sick, and ye visited me: I was in prison, and ye came to me."

The response of the righteous is revealing: "We did? When?" Jesus' answer is well known: "Inasmuch as ye have done it unto the least of these my brethren, ye have done it unto me" (Matthew 25).

Genuine humility is at heart the recognition that nothing is our own to do with as we merely please—not our money, nor our talents, nor our time, nor our selves. All are gifts from God, expressions of His creativity and generosity.

And finally it all flows back to Him. In the end there is no egotism, no hanging back, no thought of self at all, only the casting of crowns before Him and the eternal confession: "Thou art worthy, O Lord, to receive glory and honour and power. For thou hast created all things, and for thy pleasure they are and were created." Amen.

Remembering 9/11

A Moment of Silence

After the roaring and quaking, after the screaming sirens and the blaring horns, there were moments of silence.

We were struck dumb. The ordinary noisiness of our lives was muted. There were no words for what we saw on our television screens.

I live in Oregon, three thousand miles from the mass murders in New York, three thousand miles from the groans and shouts and cries of the people in Manhattan. But some of the news footage made an eerie connection in my memory.

Scenes of people burned and covered with plaster and dust stumbling away from the wreckage, pursued by a roiling cloud of smoke and dust, reminded me of the hot and poisonous cloud I had once seen rising from what was left of Mt. St. Helens. On that morning my wife and I had stood beside the road watching something beyond our ability to imagine. Mt. St. Helens had exploded.

The top of the great mountain was gone, taking

with it elk and bear, Spirit Lake, whole forests. And people. No one knew how many. No one knew what might happen next.

We didn't say much, just stood close together and tried to comprehend what we were seeing, what the great ash and sand-colored mushroom cloud boiling six miles into the sky might mean for all of us.

The air was heavy that morning, and ominously quiet. And on September 11, 2001, as I left for my office and classroom at Corban University, I felt again that strange and discomfiting quiet. Traffic on the arterial near my home was light, but what especially struck me was the silence of the skies.

For the first time in years I heard no airplanes. Not one.

Not the faint roar of big jets at 29,000 feet. Not the buzz and drone of private planes taking off and landing at the Salem Airport a couple of miles away. Nothing was in the sky but a flight of starlings and the hot, still sun. I was surprised at how accustomed I had become to the background noises of busy American life.

And now that life and the sounds that went with it had been called into question. We had been catapulted into a new era, news analysts said. We would never again be able to live the way we had.

It was easy to believe this a few days later when my wife and I drove to Portland International Airport to catch a flight to my nephew's wedding. There was no curb-side check-in, there were no visitors in the boarding area. There were policemen with dogs. The usually bustling concourse was nearly empty. And it was quiet.

Silence has been rare in our culture over the past several decades. My students have been conditioned to prefer sound—even if it's only noise—to silence. This preference is useful for people who want to sell them shirts, basketball shoes, soft drinks, cars and cosmetic surgery. Ads bombard young customers with messages that the clever messengers prefer that the buyer not think about, only respond to. Most of these messages are, of course, nonsense.

A moment's reflection will ruin the effect of expensive commercials—four and a half million dollars for a thirty-second spot during the 2015 Super Bowl. Does any young man, for example, actually believe that drinking a particular beverage will make him the center of attention of beautiful women, or that the key to social and financial success is to drive a particular automobile? Not if he stops to think about it. "Act now!" the commercials shout, and with good reason.

Silence—"dead air"—is also the horror of broadcast networks. Viewers of the 2000 PGA Championship may have been surprised at all the bird sounds coming through their television sets. Some golf fans who were also bird experts were more than surprised, since the birds that were supposedly making these sounds were not residents of Louisville, Kentucky, in August, when the tournament was played. It turned out that CBS had dubbed in the bird sounds so golf's quiet moments wouldn't be too quiet.

Silence, it seems, is not entertaining, and Americans have developed a steady craving for amusement. I don't mean to sound cranky here, and I announce without shame that I have watched my share of Seattle Mariners baseball telecasts without begrudging the loss of time to more serious pursuits.

But the writer of Ecclesiastes observes that for everything there is a season. In a sound and image drenched world there surely is a time to hit the off button, a time for quiet.

And after the horrors of September eleventh we knew this was the season.

We observed official moments of silence in the midst of traffic and of business, and before ball games.

These were gestures of sorrow and of respect for the still uncounted hundreds, our countrymen and our friends, who were dead or missing and probably dead.

And we fell silent because all this was too much to take in. We needed time to sort out our thoughts, to try to understand why this monstrous thing might have happened and what it might mean for our futures and the futures of our children.

We had to stand aside from the ordinary and casual noise of what we had come to regard as normal life, stand aside, be still and think.

We recognized, perhaps, the kind of emotional and spiritual deafness that results from the din of our plugged-in society, the amped-up environment of Walkmans and flip phones and the pounding bass of expensive car stereos.

Perhaps this is something to retrieve from the smoke and rubble of September 11—the value of a few moments of silence.

Long ago, in the quiet Judean hills with only the small sounds of night around him—the chirp of crickets, the soft bleat of a lamb—the psalmist found occasion to think carefully about what it means to be a human being created in the image of God, about his connections with the rest of creation, about God Himself.

"When I consider thy heavens," he wrote, "the work of thy fingers, what is man that thou visitest him? For thou hast made him a little lower than the angels, and hast crowned Him with glory and honor. Thou madest him to have dominion over the works of thy hands... O Lord, our Lord, how excellent is thy name in all the earth!"

We have gained, it seems to me, a new appreciation of the value of silence. Perhaps it's time to make silence—even if for only a few minutes—a more common element in our personal and corporate worship in the midst of a busy and noisy life, to "be still and know that I am God."

Ground Zero:
A Test of the Heart

August 2012

The first name is Gordon Aamoth. The last one is Igor Zukelman. There are row upon row of names, 2,792 of them. Names of people blasted, burned, and asphyxiated right here on September 11, 2001.

I am at Ground Zero with my wife, my son David, and hundreds of other people standing quietly along the length of this block, gazing through the special heavy mesh fence surrounding the great hole in the ground, clear now of debris.

"There are a lot of people here," I remark to one of the security guards at the construction entrance. "Is it often like this?"

He nods. "Every day."

In spite of all the visitors, there is not much commotion here. People speak quietly and carefully. An old man swabs at his nose with a white handkerchief. My eyes meet those of his daughter. We hold one another's gaze for a moment.

I nod slightly, meaning, *Yes, I know, this is painful for all of us, isn't it?*

Here is grief upon grief, sorrow multiplied and multiplied again. Here is a paper lei tucked into the fence's mesh, and there a single red rose, and there another.

Dozens of messages have been written on the fence in black marker pen: "God bless our New York Heroes." "We will never forget." Many of the notes are from citizens of other countries. Here is something written in Chinese, and near it a note in French. This in English: "Your Italian brothers will never forget you. God keep blessing America."

We pause before some letters scratched into the steel:

My Dad badge #34

I will never forget.

My son turns away. My wife removes her glasses, dabs at her eyes. Something in my throat feels like a hot stone, and around my heart a crust of ice forms and thickens.

I think of Zacarias Moussaoui, in jail on an immigration violation, reportedly exulting over this, and I am nearly suffocated with fury and—yes, I admit it—with hate. I wish this addled fanatic and all his terrorist tribe dead, expunged, erased from earth like a bad mistake.

Later, when I am calmer, I mention this to my son. "That's the way I feel too," he says. "I think that's natural."

It is natural. But it's not Christian.

I remember Jesus' instructions to pray for my enemies. But I do not want to do it. I tell myself I can't.

That evening David says, "I keep thinking about the people on those planes, about what the five seconds before the crash must have been like. I can't get it out of my head."

I can't, either. I remember the television footage of that unbelievable day, people diving out of windows forty stories up, choosing to be crushed on the sidewalk rather than roast to death in the great fire from which there was no escape and no rescue.

I remember the pictures of firefighters going into the burning towers and not coming out, men acting out the ultimate example of courage and duty, one of them wearing Badge #34.

I remember the towers coming down in an astonishment of smoke and ash, and a hurricane of poisonous debris sweeping up the streets of New York to engulf fleeing men and women.

And later, for days, for weeks, dogs and men and women, some with badges and some with construction union cards, risking their lives in the smoldering wreckage in search of a shoe, a tuft of hair, a finger, a charred bone to finally answer the question of those waiting to know for certain that their husbands, wives, fathers, sons, daughters, were among the 2,792.

And again I think of Moussaoui dancing and cheering as the towers come down and hundreds of Americans and others perish. Pray for him? No. I can't. He is simply too despicable, too loathsome.

But I can't find a passage in which Jesus says that I must love my enemies unless they are especially repellent, or that I must pray for those who have been spiteful except when they have been spectacularly spiteful.

People like the Ninevites, for example. There were reasons why Jonah despised them. They were brutal, dangerous, and aggressive. They heaped into great piles the heads of their conquered victims. Others they skinned and impaled outside the walls of cities to show those inside what would happen if they resisted. Jonah quite reasonably regarded them as an ongoing threat to Israel and firmly believed that the world would be better with Nineveh gone.

But God was not willing that even Nineveh should perish and He takes no pleasure in the destruction of Zacarias Moussaoui and his co-conspirators. He requires me to pray for them.

But how, exactly? What am I to ask for these people?

First, I believe I must pray that they be restrained, that no more sin be laid to their charge. I can ask this without hating them, and I can ask in sorrow rather than anger, sorrow for the victims and sorrow that human beings created in the image of God can commit such crimes and feel justified doing them. So I pray that the leaders of Al Qaeda and other terror organizations be brought to justice.

And I pray for their repentance, pray that God's mercy and love will shine on them and warm and soften their stony hearts.

Perhaps the test of my own heart is this: Do I hope to see Zacarias Moussaoui in heaven and embrace him as a brother? The answer to this question will tell whether I am becoming more like Moussaoui or more like Jesus.

Three weeks later I am home, my life resuming its routine a continent away from New York City but altered, permanently, I think, by the hour I spent at the place of horror and destruction. By all accounts Zacarias Moussaoui is unchanged, still full of hate and fury.

    I know the feeling. But I can pray for Zacarias Moussaoui, and I do, one sinner praying for another. It's starting to feel natural.

Church, Politics and Society

Christianity as Commodity

December 2003

A radio station in my city advertises its fare as round-the-clock "Christian Hits." It would be hard to find a more succinct example of my own ambivalence about what has become known as "contemporary" Christianity.

On the one hand there is much to applaud in the boldness and energy of this younger generation of Christians. They are reticent neither in their evangelism nor in their worship.

Spring missions trips to Mexico, for example, are as much a part of the college experience for many of my students and their counterparts in West Coast youth groups and colleges as the Florida and Texas beach bacchanals are for thousands of East Coast students attending secular universities. They work hard on these trips, helping construct churches and homes, assisting with Vacation Bible Schools, using their talents in drama, music and mime to introduce people to the Living Christ, playing baseball and soccer with local kids, doing whatever they are asked to do and doing it with enthusiasm and good cheer.

Their worship is equally energetic. These young people sing loudly and often. They sway, they clap, they lift their hands, they bang drums and crank up the volume on electronically amplified guitars to levels that some of their elders can't tolerate. In worship of this sort they are uninhibited and, apparently, inexhaustible.

They represent tens of thousands of mostly younger Christians crossing denominational lines as casually as they cross the Mexican border at spring break, strumming and drumming in "praise bands," swarming to Christian events—rallies, concerts, athletic demonstrations—wearing their Christianity if not on their sleeves then on their t-shirts. They are, in short, members of an easily identifiable American subculture. To some they represent the newest wave of periodic American renewals, a contemporary version of earlier Great Awakenings.

To others, however, they are a market niche, a clearly defined consumer group, a customer base to be exploited by the creators of CDs, rock bands and rap videos, as eager and as fickle in their interest in "star power" as the fans of Britney Spears and Fifty Cent.

The situation is much the same with tens of thousands of their elders, who spend millions of dollars on their own Christian CDs, and Christian luxury cruises, Christian bestsellers and special events featuring pro athletes and famous—at least among Christian evangelicals—performers and speakers.

And, as old maps used to say, here be dragons. We have entered dangerous territory, though the line of demarcation may be ill-defined. There's nothing wrong with enjoying a cruise, attending a concert, buying a CD. Experienced and skilled speakers and writers have helpful things to say, and many of us may profit from attending their seminars and reading their books.

So what's the problem? Let's call it the "commodification of Christianity." Christianity as business. Christianity as Bottom Line.

I'm not suggesting that Christian writers, singers, and speakers should not be paid for what they do. I'm not a singer, but I know from experience that writing and speaking are demanding activities, hard work that takes a lot of energy and time. Reasonable compensation is in order. And if the Gospel is spread through a variety of media, what's the problem? And if evangelical Christians are increasingly influential in entertainment, sports and politics, then just where are the alleged dragons? Is success a bad thing?

Well, no, of course not. But it has its dangers. Success defined as accession to stardom, wealth and influence, individually or corporately, may well be a definition more in accord with popular American values than with Biblical ones. And the model for success is likely to produce a parallel model of behavior.

If the church takes the corporation as its model of operations we should not be surprised when ministers think and speak of assuming a new pastorate as a "career move" or, as a friend of mine told me occurred in her own prominent and wealthy church, demand a multi-year contract as a condition of assuming the pulpit.

And if it advances entertainment as a model of Christian ministry I should not be surprised when one of my students expects me to postpone his mid-term exam because his Christian rock band has an out-of-town gig and another explains that the reason he skipped a week of classes and can't make the exam is because he has been building a course for his church's ministry to skateboarders.

Other whiffs of the dragon's breath: I am watching a local parade, part of the Iris Festival. Atop one float, sponsored by a local church, a small group, each person with on upraised arm swaying, sings over and over, "My Redeemer Lives." Good message, and I'm glad people are hearing it. At the same time I ask myself what's up with the shaggy drummer. On this chilly, overcast Oregon morning, a few cold raindrops spattering down, he's wearing a tank top. There's only one possible reason for this costume: he wants to look like a rock star, wants to *be* a rock star.

A commercial between rounds of the Friday Night Fights shows a big crowd of people waving their arms just like the folks on the float. The ad is for a set of CDs of the latest praise hits. Call this number, all major credit cards accepted. The sellers? Time Life Co.

On the front of a Christian book, a good one: "Over 250,000 copies in print!"

So here we are, conservative Christians with our own radio stations, our own television networks, our own talk shows, our own rap and rock stars, our own bestsellers, our own nationally televised music awards, our own political organizations. We now represent big market shares and powerful voting blocs. We have church growth down to a science.

But in the midst of all these trappings of success and power we would do well to pause long enough to remember Jesus' anger at those who were making merchandise of His Father's house, and His indictment of the church of the Laodiceans, who boasted, "I am rich and increased with goods, and have need of nothing," when in fact they were "wretched, and miserable, and poor, and blind and naked."

Let's remind ourselves that the Christian life begins and proceeds not with claims of power and fame, but with confessions of humility and weakness.

"God be merciful to me, a sinner."

"He must increase, but I must decrease."

There's nothing flattering or glamorous about this kind of talk. It doesn't describe a marketable image. But it's the only way to bring to maturity our redeemed character, the only way, the Bible says, to be conformed not to the image of General Motors or the Disney Corporation or MCA, but to the image of Christ.

Garage Sale of the Mind
2009

Several years ago while getting ready for work, I enjoyed some quick calculations about how much money I'd have at retirement, more than I would have imagined.

"Let's see, ten more years at 14.5 percent per annum like this year, and—wow! Not bad for a guy who knows more about Walt Whitman than about Wall Street." I'd be financially secure, not wealthy by American standards, but certainly comfortable. Probably enough cash for a cruise or two, a couple of weeks in an over-water bure in Tahiti, a place I've wanted to see since reading *Mutiny on the Bounty* years ago, maybe a visit to Wordsworth's cottage in England's Lake District...

And I didn't even have to do anything—just watch the numbers rise as my paper wealth grew by the month. What fun!

As the Trix cereal ads used to say, "Silly rabbit." Had I forgotten all the history I'd read, history that included accounts of repeated economic downturns following periods of overheated growth? Well, no, but I enjoyed reading economists who assured us that with the advent of the microchip, the game was different. The old cycles had given way to unending economic growth.

And maybe to some degree I had begun to ignore what I knew most deeply: the dangers that accrue when our appetite for acquisition brings about a kind of economic obesity.

Jesus warned about giving our lives over to the pursuit of stuff— "bigger barns" in the parable recorded by Luke—all the while forgetting that our goods are not us, that they can easily disappear, and that trading our lives for things is a foolish bargain.

Thoreau, conducting his "experiment in living" at Walden Pond, observed that the cost of something is the amount of life required to be given in exchange for it, and asked, "Shall we always study to obtain more…and not sometimes be content with less?" In his chapter titled "Economy" he pointed out that when we have "obtained those things which are necessary to life, there is another alternative than to obtain the superfluities."

Bill McKibben, writing in the November 2008

issue of *Harper's,* points out that "the only thing we've asked of our economy for a century has been growth, and it's gotten us in a world of trouble."

I'm no economist, but I suspect Mr. McKibben is onto something. If all we want is more, then we had better expect to pay the price of a degraded environment, of rising noise levels, of work schedules stretched beyond what God intended, of absent and exhausted parents.

The consequence of inexhaustible expectations confronting exhaustible resources of time, energy, and raw material is sure to create a rising tide of anxiety and discontent. Paul had no such anxiety. He noted that he had sometimes had plenty, sometimes little, and in whatever circumstances had learned "to be content."

I'm going to take a deep breath now...and suggest that what is true for individuals and municipalities can also be true of churches. I'm pretty sure that I'm not the only person who knows of at least one church that has been wrecked by an overly ambitious building plan. At a time when some members of the congregation have lost pensions and jobs, it seems appropriate for churches, too, to take a careful look at their corporate spending habits. Maybe they are all in order, but I don't think we should assume so without checking. Does every new church need a gym? Can we get along without that coffee bar we had planned for our new wing?

I wonder if we American Christians have not grown accustomed to a life of luxury that is not so different from the life valued by any other prosperous American, the one advertised as the good life by people who want to sell us things.

For example, I'm uneasy at the ads I see in Christian magazines for Christian cruises. They look pretty much like the ads I see in all the travel magazines: extraordinarily good-looking people—models, I should think—very well dressed, and gleaming tables laden with the best food money can buy.

I am not opposed to cruises; my wife wants to take the inside passage to Alaska, and I hope we can do it one of these summers. But how did luxury cruises become a thread woven into the tapestry of a supposedly distinctive Christian system of values and behavior?

In the midst of the flood of news about failing banks and the recklessness of huge mortgage lenders, maybe it's time for me to be content with less: less space, less travel, fewer dinners out. And, given the very real poverty facing some people in a period of heavy job layoffs, to make more contributions to my church's food bank.

Maybe it's a good time for all of us to have a garage sale of the mind and spirit, to sort out who we are and what we most profoundly want and need, to let go of some of the gaudy economic furniture that has cluttered our lives and our thinking.

Maybe it's a good time for a wealthy and politically powerful American church to make sure we are not like the church in Laodicea, who boasted, "I am rich, have become wealthy, and have need of nothing," when in fact they were "wretched, miserable, poor, blind, and naked." To them God said, "Anoint your eyes with eye salve, that you may see" (Revelation 3:17-18).

It's likely that this economic crisis will force some changes upon many of us, will at the least require us to take another look at the way we have grown accustomed to living. And maybe that's not a bad thing at all.

Courtesy

The cheerful Cornish woman who had checked us into our room at the old hotel waved as my wife and I started down the narrow path leading to The Haven and the ruins of Tintagel. "If yer not back by dinner, we'll know that Merlin got ye!" she admonished us with a laugh.

We were in the land of King Arthur and the Knights of the Round Table. According to other old tales, it was also the ancient seat of Mark, King of Cornwall, uncle of Sir Tristan, one of Arthur's knights.

And it was the story of Tristan, as retold by Joseph Bedier, that played again in my memory as I gazed down into The Haven, the harbor where Tristan's ship arrived bearing Iseult, the Irish beauty who was to be King Mark's wife.

It was easy to imagine the scene: the ship being rowed into the narrow Haven, people lining the castle walls cheering and waving, the boat docking near the now-ruined gate that guarded the path that led to the upper gate and opened into the castle's courtyard.

"As King Mark came down to greet Iseult upon the shore," the old tale reports, "Tristan took her hand and led her to the King and the King...led her in great pomp to his castle... And as she came in the hall amid the vassals, her beauty shone so that the walls were lit as they are lit at dawn." In its poetry and ceremony, the royal court of kings in Britain reflected the customs and expectations of a culture sensitive to status.

From this—the manners and the speech of the court—we derive our word "courtesy," a character trait in short supply today, but certainly one that ought to characterize the children of the King of Kings.

Courtesy is not merely a matter of etiquette, although it sometimes includes expectations of appropriate dress or ceremonies of the table: what to do with a napkin, which fork to use first, where to lay down a knife. Courtesy has more to do with speaking and behaving in ways that reflect our consideration for others and for their comfort and dignity.

For Christians, courtesy involves recognizing that other people—as well as we—are created in God's image and are the objects of His love and care. In a society in which "self-esteem" has become an unquestioned value, we do well to remind ourselves that Scripture commands us to esteem others better than ourselves (Philippians 2:1-8).

This doesn't mean that we should fail to exercise the gifts, talents, and strengths that God has given us. The Lord expects us to appreciate and use our gifts in worshipful and joyful ways. False humility is as obnoxious an evidence of an inflated ego as outright arrogance is.

Courtesy means that we remain alert to the well-being of others and to the ways we might foster it. This is to say that we are ready, as a habit, to recognize the worth of others. Often this means attention to what may be supposed to be the little things—the way we sound on the phone, the way we drive, the way we speak to a sales associate when we shop, the way we recognize good service with a tip.

One of my colleagues helped pay his undergraduate tuition by waiting tables at a mid-level restaurant. He hadn't been on the job long when an experienced waitress told him, "Don't expect much of a tip from that table. They prayed."

"Was she right?" I asked him.

"Yeah," he said ruefully. "People who prayed or who looked as if they had just come from church had the reputation of being cheap tippers, and I'm sorry to say that in my experience the reputation seemed deserved. Now, if I can't afford a good tip, I don't go."

To people of no special status, a poor tip is demeaning, a sign of disrespect, of being held in low regard. Remember the regard Christ showed for people whom others despised.

Christians are commanded to live by a sense of community that is blind to personal wealth, name, or social position (James 2:1-9). Simon, the Pharisee who invited Jesus to dinner, didn't choose to show to the itinerant rabbi the courtesies he probably would have offered if he had thought Jesus was more than a curiosity. It was left to a woman of scandalous reputation to recognize Jesus as the One sent from God and to honor Him with her attention (Luke 7:36-50).

One of the problems in the carnal church at Corinth was simple rudeness, the failure of the well-to-do to treat their less prosperous and noteworthy brothers and sisters with respect. The prosperous Christians seemed to share the view of their wealthy pagan neighbors toward the low status of poor fellow Christians. Their casual lack of courtesy, said Paul, made even the celebration of the Lord's Supper unpleasant and divisive.

Jesus teaches us something else. What we do to the least of His brethren, He said, we do to Him (Matthew 25:40). If we knew it was Jesus taking our dinner order, or driving the car in front of us, or checking our bags at the airport, how would we speak of or to Him? We are people of the Court, attendants of the High King of heaven. There is great dignity in this, a dignity that we must recognize in our dealings with one another and with those who have not yet received the Good News.

The great walls of the ancient British kings are now ruins, the roofs collapsed, the floors of chapel and armory and banquet hall grown over with grass. But the reign of the Kings of Kings will never cease.

We are His ambassadors. We do well, then, to make certain that our actions and our speech are always "with grace, seasoned with salt," reflecting the power and grace of the eternal King Whom we represent and serve.

Apples of Gold in Settings of Silver

"What's in all these boxes?" the guy at the freight dock asked.

"Books."

"Books? All these boxes? Books?"

I nodded.

"Whose are they?"

"Mine. I'm shipping them to my new home in Oregon."

"They're all yours? Have you actually read them all?"

"Most of them," I said. "Some more than once. I'm a teacher. Carpenters have lots of hammers and saws. Plumbers have wrenches. I have books. They're my tools."

It was a good enough answer as far as it went. It was plain, judging from his raised eyebrows and brief shake of his head, that the man was not in a frame of mind to hear the rest of it: that these were the resonant voices of our civilization, the voices that have shaped our political ideas, explored the perplexities, ironies and delights of human experience, and created in our minds and memories Camelot and Narnia and the palace of Kubla Khan.

He was not the last to squint a skeptical eye in the direction of my books or on the very notion of spending so much time with the printed page. To some, reading is suspiciously akin to idleness. It doesn't appear to them that readers are working. Others take the opposing view: reading is too hard. Why not wait for the video version?

There are many answers to these objections. Here are some.

Reading is an act of humility. When we read we acknowledge that there is more to know, that we do not regard our ignorance with satisfaction. When we pick up a book we consent to having our prejudices questioned and our unexamined assumptions challenged. "The greater part of what my neighbors call good I believe…to be bad," wrote Thoreau, that prickly Yankee, in the midst of his "experiment in living" at Walden Pond, and a thoughtful person, especially one claiming citizenship in the New Jerusalem, might profit from time spent mulling over that writer's radical critique of popular American values.

Essayist and poet X. J. Kennedy writes, "To leap over the wall of self, to look through another's eyes—this is valuable experience, which literature offers." For the Christian reader this surely must be part of what it means to love one's neighbor as oneself, for love must acknowledge the dignity and worth of the other, those living and those no longer among us. Literature, said Nobel laureate Saul Bellow, is a "conversation with the dead," elder voices that demand our ear.

Similarly, reading multiplies our lives. "You want to live everywhere," my wife once remarked. She was exaggerating, but she wasn't far off. Perhaps my only regret about the Pacific Northwest is that living here means I can't live in New England or Montana's Mission Valley or South Florida or the coast of Northern California. There's only one me, and only one lifetime.

But reading lets me escape the ordinary boundaries of time and place. "There is no frigate like a book," Emily Dickinson wrote, "to bear us lands away." So I have hunted blackbuck on the African plains with Hemingway, explored the polar icecap with Shackleton, steamed the Mississippi with Mark Twain, sailed the "wine-dark seas" with Odysseus, and listened to the apostle Paul address the Athenian philosophers at Mars' Hill.

Put another way, reading improves our understanding by providing perspective. Other minds, other lives, other voices, other times and places are necessary to help us measure and balance our own.

Justifiable pride in our national heritage, for example, may be tempered and sobered when we read Frederick Douglass's "What to the Slave is the Fourth of July?" or experience the terror of WWI Allied artillery with a twenty-year old German infantryman in *All Quiet on the Western Front.*

And whatever our view of the rightness or wrongness of choosing to end WWII by using atomic weapons, John Hersey's *Hiroshima* reminds us that there were actual human beings at ground zero the day the sky turned to fire.

Those of us who have made reading a habit have found in literature the words that we needed but could not ourselves compose, poems articulating our own sorrows and loves and worship.

Standing at the bedside of an uncle dying of cancer, I was glad for the prayers in *The Book of Common Prayer.* They said what I would have said if I could have thought of the words, and if my throat had not had stuck in it a bone of tired grief.

When one of my students, the daughter of a friend, died suddenly and unexpectedly, it helped somehow to take as my own the elegy that Theodore Roethke had written for a gifted student killed in a fall from a horse:

Over this damp grave I speak the words of my love,
I with no rights in this matter,
Neither father nor lover.

On happier occasions lovers have, with Elizabeth Barrett Browning, counted the ways of love, or remembered Lord Byron's tribute:

She walks in beauty like the night
of cloudless climes and starry skies.

Too, great poets have provided readers enduring expressions of worship, vibrant in imagination and skill, and refreshingly original.

Here's Gerard Manley Hopkins:
Glory be to God for dappled things—
For skies of couple-colour as a brindled cow;
For rose-moles all in stipple upon trout that swim;
Fresh-firecoal chestnut falls; finches' wings...

All these mixed things, and more, Hopkins reminds us,

> *He fathers-forth whose beauty is past change:*
> *Praise him.*

Christian—and non-Christian—poets remind us of the sacredness of what we may in our carelessness have come to regard as ordinary. "A mouse," mused Walt Whitman, "is miracle enough to stagger sextillions of infidels." And E. E. Cummings asked,

> *how should tasting touching hearing seeing*
> *breathing any—lifted from the no*
> *of all nothing—human merely being*
> *doubt unimaginable You?*

And it's hardly surprising that reading widely makes us better hearers of the Word. After all, God has chosen to speak to us in a book, an anthology of letters, narratives, poems, and, in "The Song of Solomon" and "Job," something very like drama. If we are unfamiliar with these forms, the human forms God chose for the divine message, it is unlikely that we will be able to read the Bible in the fullest ways it was meant to be understood.

"A word fitly spoken," says the proverb, "is like apples of gold in settings of silver." And when these words are written down they are a treasure to be passed from generation to generation, a treasure to be shared and multiplied, as undiminished by use as the widow's oil.

I sit, as I write, surrounded by books, the lifelong labors of historians, dramatists, novelists and poets. From the west wall, above a bookcase packed with the words of Sophocles, Aristotle, Shakespeare, Milton and Pascal, my grandfather's pensive gaze rests upon me. In his hand is a book. I keep that portrait by the door to remind me to keep my eyes open, to pay attention, to listen carefully. His steady eyes tell me I have a lot to learn.

"Are all these books yours?" new students sometimes ask. Well, they are if I read them. They can be theirs, too, occasions of instruction and delight, if they have ears to hear. I hope they do. Their grandchildren and their grandchildren's civilization depend upon it.

Dressing for Christian Success

From time to time my wife lays down the law. "That thing has got to go!" she orders, holding a shapeless shirt or a baggy pair of pants between her index finger and thumb as if it were something the dog might have rolled in.

The rest of the conversation might go like this:

"But—but I've worn that for years. It's like a part of me."

"I know you have. Too many years. Look at this collar. The points are getting bare. See these cuffs? And you already own old shirts for cutting wood. This thing is an embarrassment. It's got to go."

Christmas Day may well find a new blazer or, recently, a new suit hanging in my closet. My wife wants to make sure I'm presentable when I walk into my office and classroom.

I've learned not to mix checks and stripes, not to wear a green tie with a blue shirt. And with each sports coat in my closet I hang two or three ties that I know work with them. Each combination represents a deliberate, considered choice that has passed a benevolent but firm inspection.

Books and seminars offer advice on dressing for success, explaining to job applicants and job holders alike how to choose clothing that suggests maturity, competence, and respect for superiors, co-workers and clients.

Scripture too has instructions for clothing ourselves—not on choosing a sweater or a sports coat or a suit—but on choosing clothing for the inner man. And in Colossians chapter three Paul makes it clear that our attitudes and behaviors lie within our power to choose.

Some years ago a United States President embarrassed himself and humiliated his wife, even facing impeachment, over bad behavior with a young intern and then lying about it. Many people wondered how an intelligent man could do something not only immoral but astonishingly stupid.

One answer was advanced in an article written by an evolutionary psychologist explaining that, like other mammals, members of the homo sapiens group simply act out of a kind of genetic memory, the consequence of eons of evolution. The President, this writer claimed, was simply doing what the big bull in the herd always does, what evolution more or less compels him to do: pass along superior DNA to all the females in the herd. Behavior that some might call arrogant and immoral, wrong on all counts, was really quite natural, something programmed into the human animal in pretty much the same way that cats are programmed to kill gophers or dogs to mark their territory.

Scripture says otherwise. In Colossians Paul admonishes Christians to make deliberate choices about how we are to present ourselves before other people and before God.

"Put off the old man," he writes. And what follows is a list of the ugly, dirty clothing we need to banish from our inner closets, stuff that never fits, that suits no occasion, that nobody wants to see.

Let's check our closet, then, and throw out anger. Remember the last time you said something remarkably wise when you were red-faced with anger? Neither do I. More likely, when we allow an angry outburst we'll recall it with red-faced embarrassment. Proverbs 22:24 warns against even keeping company with a bad-tempered man. He's trouble. And if we're the one with the hair-trigger temper, Paul says that we need to decide that it has to go.

Another old rag is rage, dangerous anger that may well result in violence. I think of a man I had as a student in a night class at a nearby prison. He was not a habitual criminal; he'd been a dairy farmer. He was big, probably 6'2" and 250 pounds, and one night an argument with his wife escalated, and he beat her to death. "I hadn't planned to kill her," he told me, "but that was in there somewhere."

Is rage in your closet? Better get rid of it before something terrible and ugly happens.

And here's malice, wishing someone ill, taking pleasure in someone else's misfortune. The great poet John Milton imagines in "Paradise Lost" Satan, ejected from heaven, taking malicious pleasure in subverting and wrecking Eden. I suspect Milton was right in identifying malice as a chief motive impelling The Evil One. It's certainly not a garment suitable for the New Man.

Next on the list of throwaways is slander, one expression of malice. It is spreading evil, malicious speech, injuring someone by talking about him in ways intended to harm. Slanderers go beyond gossip. Gossip, while damaging, may at least be true. Slanderers insist, for example, that President Obama is a Muslim, in spite of his insistence that he is not and in the absence of any evidence that he is. These folks don't merely disagree with the President, they find perverse pleasure in saying something politically injurious even if untrue.

Filthy language, which may include slander, and lying, another kind of filthy language, conclude Paul's Colossians list of ugly stuff to be dumped. We can choose to throw these things out.

But the closet is not to be left empty. "Clothe yourselves," Paul exhorts in Colossians 3:12. And then he identifies a whole new wardrobe. Just as we choose garments from our drawers and closets to make ourselves physically presentable, we are to dress the new inner man every morning with carefully chosen clothing.

Pick out compassion. Compassion is an action of holy imagination that takes us out of ourselves and places us inside the world of another. Compassion sees the difficulties and pain of others, and acts to help. Jesus was the friend of sinners like despised Zacchaeus. And an adulterous woman whom some were eager to stone. He was not too busy to heal blind and crippled beggars. He touched lepers whom no one else would touch. He wept with friends at the tomb of their brother. People who want to be like Jesus can begin by choosing compassion as a basic item to put on.

The next three pieces of clothing—humility, gentleness and patience—go well together, and they coordinate with compassion. They all show that the wearer has removed himself from the center of his own attention. There's nothing flashy about humility, gentleness, and patience. Quite the opposite. Like all good clothing, this rich apparel does not draw attention to itself. But it fits perfectly, and lends the wearer grace and freedom.

Dressed in these clothes we will be prepared to follow Paul's next admonition: Bear with one another. We sometimes get on one another's nerves. Paul tells us to overlook these irritations, to make allowances, to cut one another some slack.

And, he says, we are to forgive the grievances we may have, even when they are genuine. Elsewhere Scripture says that followers of Jesus are to be easily entreated, quick to accept apologies.

On June 2, 2010, pitcher Armando Gallaraga of the Detroit Tigers was one out away from a perfect game. It would have been only the twenty-first in baseball history. With two out in the ninth inning, Gallaraga made a good pitch which the Cleveland hitter grounded to the right side of the infield. The Tigers' first baseman backhanded the ball up and tossed it to Gallaraga, who was hustling over to cover first. The runner was clearly out, but umpire Jim Joyce waved "Safe!" and the perfect game was gone.

When Joyce saw the replay later, he went to the Tigers' locker room in tears, found the pitcher, and apologized. Gallaraga quietly accepted the apology, and the next day brought the Tigers' lineup to the plate ump, Jim Joyce. The men shook hands and cemented a friendship based on forgiveness. Detroit fans applauded something more important than a perfect game, more important than baseball.

And over all these things, Paul says, "put on love." Perhaps we can think of this as a kind of coat that coordinates perfectly with the rest of our clothing.

So let's throw out the ugly things that tear apart friendships, teams, churches, and marriages—all the torn, smelly ragged stuff that can too easily fill up our closets. We're not forced to wear this stuff.

God says to choose a different wardrobe, one that is becoming, tailored by the One who wants us to match the image of His Son.

A Welcome for the Heroes

Summer 2013

The marquee on the Tower Theater read WELCOME HOME! ASHTON EATON WORLD'S GREATEST ATHLETE. And what a welcome it was.

My wife, Bonnie, and I and our daughter Cathy and her two little girls, Morgan and Madeleine, were gathered with several thousand others on the sidewalks of downtown Bend, a city of 80,000 at the eastern front of Oregon's Cascade Mountain Range. Bend's location and sunny climate invite outdoor activity—hiking, biking, fishing, skiing. In Bend physical fitness is a civic virtue. In the summer even the police wear shorts.

And now fire engines and classic cars led a parade through streets lined with fluttering American flags to honor the fittest of the fit, a local boy, Ashton Eaton, Olympic gold medalist and world record holder in the decathlon, ten events run over two exhausting days testing an athlete's speed, strength and endurance in sprints, hurdles, throws, jumps, and finally a 1500-meter run. The winner of the Olympic decathlon is generally regarded as the world's best all-around athlete.

Bonnie and I were visiting Cathy and her family, just moved from San Francisco. We had learned of the parade and joined the excited locals as the band playing "The Stars and Stripes Forever" rounded the corner. Two 1920s vintage cars carried young Eaton's grandparents. And here came a Corvette convertible, Eaton's renowned coach perched atop the back seat.

A cheer rose from the crowd for the great coach, but he pointed behind him and shouted, "There's Ashton!"

And here he came, chiseled, lean and handsome, striding through the town wearing a green University of Oregon t-shirt, his gold medal around his neck, grinning and waving at the cheering, clapping crowd.

Morgan hopped up and down as though her feet were hot. Bonnie snapped photos. And as the great athlete moved on down Wall Street we could follow his progress by the applause swelling like surf.

The parade halted in front of the theater, and there were speeches. Eaton's mother dabbed at her eyes and thanked the town for its support of her son. Ashton held up his medal. "This is mine," he said. "I won it. But it's yours, too." And he, too, spoke of the support he had always felt from the people of Central Oregon.

Then it was the mayor's turn. He presented Eaton with a large plaque with a gold key attached, the key to the city, an acknowledgement of the young man's importance to the city of Bend and the nearby towns and ranches.

Even though I was a visitor from the other side of the mountains, I was glad to be part of this joyful event, an appropriate recognition not just of a gold medal, but of the hundreds and thousands of hours of intense and often painful training—hour upon hour, day upon day—of sessions in the weight room, lap upon lap of interval training that leaves runners exhausted and gasping, sprint after sprint down the runways of the long jump and pole vault, throw after straining throw of discus, javelin, and heavy shot, mile after mile of distance training to build endurance for the 1500-meter run.

There were no crowds then, no cheers, no band, no speeches, no excited children. Only a coach and an athlete, Ashton Eaton, laboring hard and faithfully toward the prize, Olympic gold.

Last summer my friend Dave Johnson, who

somehow won an Olympic decathlon bronze medal while competing with a broken foot—to my mind one of the most amazing and courageous athletic feats ever—flew to Germany for a reunion of former Olympic decathlon medalists. The great Americans were there—Milt Campbell, Rafer Johnson, Bill Toomey, Bruce Jenner—along with their friends and rivals from other countries. The men ate together, laughed and reminisced about the great competitions among the world's greatest athletes.

And in November I was in Germany, too, to teach a compressed two-week course in literature for a study abroad program for Christian college students called AMBEX (American-Bavarian Exchange).

As part of our study we went to Nuremburg, where a document center and museum stand on the site of the great Nazi Party rally of 1934, recorded in the world's first propaganda film, Leni Riefenstahl's "Triumph of the Will," a film frightening in its power and persuasiveness, extolling Hitler and his program to inaugurate a thousand-year Reich, a world order to be established and controlled by those who wanted to believe they were part of a superior race.

I stood not far from the zeppelin air field where thousands of Nazis carrying torches had marched and assembled to listen in rapt silence to their glaring, gesticulating fuhrer. "Ein Volk," a banner read. 'Ein Fuhrer." One people. One leader.

And the film showed Hitler at a daylight rally, strutting past multitudes frantic with adoration, past ranks of grim troops who later swore allegiance not to Germany but to the fuhrer himself. He stood above them on a high platform at the end of the great arena as they roared over and over, "Sieg—Heil! Sieg—Heil! Sieg—Heil!" Victory! Hail!

The lie he told was an old one, the very oldest: You will be like gods. And the result was the same as ever: death.

"The last shall be first," Jesus said, and as I looked at the crumbling remains of arrogant evil I thought of Vachel Lindsay's poem in which he imagines William Booth, the founder of the Salvation Army, leading a company of earthly misfits into heaven. They are not powerful and they are not pretty. The Nazis would have worked them to death or sent them straightway to the gas.

But of such is the kingdom of heaven. The beggars and the homeless are guests at the wedding feast that the proud have spurned. And in Lindsay's vision, as they parade through the Holy City and approach their waiting Lord and Savior they are transformed, made anew—the misshapen, bent and twisted bodies changed into "athletes clean." Maybe into bodies like an Olympic champion's.

Thousands in London watched Ashton Eaton win gold, and millions more watched on television. His name was on every sports page and in every sports show on television. Months later in a small city in Oregon he signed autograph after autograph. There's nothing wrong with any of that. He had earned our appreciation and admiration.

But I suspect there will be celebrations in heaven for heroes few of us have heard of: believers even now meeting in secret, defying those who hate the Gospel of Jesus Christ; pastors around the world quietly and faithfully caring for the flock entrusted to them; those who have given up jobs rather than compromise their Christian ethics; my friends Bruce and Diana, who have given their lives and love to a daughter born without part of her brain, who would never be able to tell them she loved them, never sing or fix herself a slice of toast or brush her teeth, a girl some would have given over to institutional care.

Heroes. And not just until the next Olympiad. Heroes for eternity.

The Courage of Everlasting Life

Summer 1995

"Would you sign our petition?" the lady outside the library asked. She had a sweet, grandmotherly face, and was quietly dressed. I appreciated her interest in Oregon's long tradition of the use of the Initiative, but no, I would not lend my name to this effort: the sign on her table read "Death with Dignity."

It's an appealing title, one which purports to offer a humane alternative to images of emaciated, comatose old people fettered unwillingly and perhaps unwittingly by wires and tubes to a hospital bed and to an artificially prolonged existence, their hearts and lungs operating by neither their own power nor volition.

So why would anybody be opposed to a natural death, if that is what "death with dignity" promises? Because the real agenda of this movement is something different. "Death with dignity" is code for assisted suicide, and the discussion about who should be assisted to death is based on what some call "quality of life." The lives of those who have suffered serious physical or mental impairment may be determined by themselves, or by a legal and medical committee, to be no longer worthy of the normal protection of the law. Neither the impaired persons nor their doctors nor their families need accept continued responsibility for low-quality lives other than to end them quickly and painlessly.

This is not simply theoretical. One of the users of Jack Kevorkian's "suicide machine" was an Oregon woman who, though in present good health, had been diagnosed with progressive Alzheimer's disease. Rather than suffer years of physical and mental deterioration and drain her husband's bank account and energy on long-term care she took Kevorkian's way out.

I thought of her as I made my way to the library's parking lot. I tried to imagine the dismay of a bright, active woman facing the prospect of losing her memory, her ability to read, to think, to act, and ultimately of losing control even of bowel and bladder. I could understand, perhaps, why she might rather die.

But I thought, too, of Marchant King and Herbert Hotchkiss, my old teachers, men who endured years of infirmity without complaint, who served the

Lord with grace and power even as their bodies shriveled and failed.

More than twenty years before I sat in his classroom Dr. King had been told that the degenerative disease that was weakening his legs would soon cripple and kill him.

By the time I knew Dr. Marchant King he had long outlived the doctor's predictions, though he had been forced, in time, to submit first to crutches, then to a wheelchair. But the force of his personality, the acuteness and energy of his mind, and the intensity of his commitment to Jesus Christ and His work made the "handicapped" label ludicrous. He couldn't walk, that was all.

In his chair he studied long hours, did the household shopping and even raked his lawn. In the classroom he delivered lectures that made fifty minutes seem but a moment. A glance or a nod terrified the slacker and urged on the conscientious. He was the patriarch of a brilliant family: his wife and son both held Ph.D.s and chaired college departments, and his daughter was a surgeon.

Across the hall from Dr. King's office was the office of his old Princeton Seminary classmate, Herbert Hotchkiss. Together they had left Princeton for the new Westminster Seminary when it became clear that Princeton had chosen a theological stance that the two young men could not support and did not wish to be identified with.

Dr. Hotchkiss was old Ivy League, his advanced degrees in engineering and literature from Cornell reflective of his range of interests and expertise. He was a knowledgeable amateur botanist and had been a naval officer and a pastor, a man of astonishing vigor of mind and body.

And then one day a small bomb exploded in his head. The stroke damaged his hearing and thickened and slowed his speech. By the time I met him heart problems had impaired his circulation, slowing his step and making it difficult for him to stay awake in a chair.

He had his own answer for this. He had his son-in-law build a stand-up desk, at which he labored far into the night on the papers he demanded of us every Friday, correcting our grammar, pointing out inconsistencies of thought, excising clichés, and commending the occasional well-built paragraph or fresh metaphor.

He worked late, too, to make sure his lectures were fresh and up-to-date. When someone asked why he spent so much preparation time on courses he had taught for twenty years he peered out from under his bushy eyebrows and explained, "I want my students to drink from a moving stream, not a stagnant pond."

And when, finally, he was too deaf to hear the sermon and too weary to stay awake to the final "amen," he came to church anyway, every Sunday. He'd been retired, but had not lost his sense of mission for college students. Each Sunday he chose one of the students in the service to pray for as long as he could stay awake.

They are both gone, now—in God's time, not Jack Kevorkian's. I can scarcely imagine their response if someone had suggested the poison pill to them: perhaps a roar and a clap of thunder, or an earthquake. For these men had the courage of everlasting life, a kind of courage that set them apart.

I've thought hard about what I saw in these men, about the nature of their nobility and courage. I believe that what I saw stemmed from three things: their commitment to principle, their devotion to a cause, and their recognition that the story of their lives was to be written by God, not they themselves or other human beings.

Like the three Hebrew children in the book of Daniel, their commitment to principle banished fear. A commitment to principle does not allow us to ask if a course of action is easy or difficult, comfortable or painful—only if it's right.

Like great athletes or soldiers, my old teachers had set aside questions of their own comfort for the sake of a greater cause. An athlete intent on the game simply has no time for fear. He ignores pain, weariness and danger in his quest for the prize. As with all virtues, courage is a form of self-forgetfulness.

And with Joshua, Gideon and David, professors Hotchkiss and King recognized that the battle is the Lord's, that once we have done our duty He controls the outcome. He will bring down the walls, scatter the enemy, topple the giant. Our labor will not be in vain. These two men knew their Bible, and this knowledge, with their own experiences of God's faithfulness, gave them courage and a force of character that was heroic.

When some people think of courage they think of linebackers, of firefighters, of test pilots. I think of two white-haired old friends, one deaf and limping, the other in a wheelchair, but warriors still, old lions, fearless as fire. Theirs was—and is—life with dignity.

The New View

Summer 2011

Like most people we have always considered our back yard to be *our* yard, an increasingly important retreat as the neighborhood around us changed. The house was built in the sixties on the last street inside the city limits. Across the street lay green fields, and beyond them forested hills rolled away toward the Cascade Mountains.

By the time we bought the house a manufactured-home park, extravagantly named Meadowlark Manor, enclosed the north and east sides of the property.

Still, across the road were fields of corn and beans and pumpkins, and to the west of our lot lay a meadow, and since the area was zoned agricultural-residential we figured our little patch of relative peace was secure.

We were wrong. The meadow is gone, in its place a three-story apartment complex. How is that in keeping with the zoning designation, I asked city officials at the planning hearing.

The answer: Well, it's going to be for farm workers. As it turns out, the Colonia Libertad apartments are reserved for Hispanic families, few of whom are actually employed on farms. I suspect that the primary reason for the new zoning ruling was an influx of federal money—other people's money—cash that municipalities find irresistible. And across the road the corn, beans and pumpkins are giving way to warehouses.

Our Spanish-speaking neighbors are pleasant and tidy, but with upper-story windows looming over our back yard we felt crowded and exposed.

And then last year our neighbors on the east side pointed out that roots from our big Douglas fir and even bigger sequoia were buckling their driveway. I loved those big trees and the green screen they provided, but clearly they had outgrown their space, dropping loads of needles and once, during an ice storm, heavy limbs onto Ray and Marlene's roof. The trees would have to come down.

For two days the retired folks from Meadowlark Manor gathered in lawn chairs to watch the crew from R and R Tree Service bring down the big trees, especially the great sequoia.

The first day an agile and amazingly strong young man climbed to the top, began chain-sawing limbs, and worked his way down, sometimes holding on with one hand and running the heavy chain saw with the other. The second day he began sawing through the bare trunk, lowering thick slices of wood by rope. Finally there was a ten-foot section that he dropped into the back yard.

There was a great whump. Our house shook, and dishes flew out of the china cabinet. And our great tree was gone.

We had knee-deep drifts of pinkish-brown sawdust, and I invited the spectators to take all they wanted as mulch for their flower beds. Lawn chairs were put away and wheelbarrows appeared.

Eventually the tree trunks, stumps and sawdust were gone, and we had to decide what to do about the chewed-up denuded ground that had once been the soft, shady earth beneath the big trees. The entire east side of the house lay completely exposed.

What could we do to restore the shady privacy we had always enjoyed? Putting in trees tall enough to do the job was too expensive, and even though the stumps of our old trees had been ground down to just below the surface they took up so much area that our planting options were limited. I was not happy.

And then my perspective changed. One of the folks from Meadowlark strolled by, looked into the back yard and stayed to chat.

That back yard shows the results of a decade of hard work. I don't like yard work, but my wife loves to garden and I love her, so I've spent a lot more time planting and weeding and pruning than I otherwise would.

Now the woman from down the street took in the orange eruption of giant poppies, the crimson peonies, the trees, the trumpet vine, the fuchsias, the rhodies and a dozen other flowering plants. "We don't have much to offer you," she said, looking over her shoulder at the modest plantings along her street, "but for us, looking into your yard, it's like the Garden of Eden."

And now I saw that my efforts to keep eyes out had been a mistake. Maybe I should think how to invite eyes in. Americans like privacy, and I probably like it more than most, but my neighbor's gratitude for the view into my property and her reference to God's creative gift to the first humans compelled me to wonder if my desire to enclose myself in greenery was the most Christian way to think about our landscaping plans.

Perhaps it wasn't.

The next day I stepped outside the gate of the chain link fence and looked at my property from the neighbors' perspective. What—and where—might Bonnie and I plant that could please the eye of the mostly older folks out for their walk-for-health?

And all that newly bare ground and naked chain link fence between us and Ray and Marlene? They were going to see the area as much as we were, so we decided to invite them to be part of the planning.

Marlene loved the forsythia we put in. The vivid yellow blooms would offer early cheer to Oregon's usual gray March. I had intended to plant morning glory to cover a section of exposed fence. "Please don't," she said, worried that the vine might spread into her own flower bed. Okay, then, how about pink jasmine?

She was delighted. "That will smell so good," she said. And she was pleased to see that the scrawny lilac that had barely survived under the shade of the sequoia was exuberant with new foliage.

Charles, our neighbor to the north, frail and short of breath, likes the new Japanese maple, and when the sweet peas are grown along one section of fence he'll be able to see them from his porch. His son Chuck was hit by a car some months ago, and our old but serviceable spa offers some relief from pain in his broken leg.

Our yard, of course, is nothing like the Garden of Eden, but our neighbor's appreciative comment has prompted us to consider how we think about our green yard, and how we plan it. Genesis indicates that God's garden was a gift to human beings, an invitation to peace and joy and beauty.

And our garden, too, is His. The sun and the rain and the sprouting seed are His gift to us. If our yard and garden serve as an invitation to our neighbors to find delight in God's beauty and generosity, we've planned it right.

"Ooh, bonita," our Guatamalan neighbor from Colonia Libertad said as Bonnie showed her around, filling Evangelina's hands with rosemary and mint and bright red dahlias.

"The earth is the Lord's," the psalmist reminds us, and it's important to remember that His ownership doesn't stop at our fence. We're working to open our garden views to people around us who need to experience some of His fullness and joy.

Reasonable Service

"I can tell Americans when they get off the plane," said my friend Sue, home for a visit. She had been living in Israel. "You can tell by the way they walk."

"How's that?" I asked.

"Arrogant," she said. "Like they own the place."

"Do I walk like that?"

She looked at me levelly. "Of course you do. You're an American."

I asked Jorge, one of my students, about this. Jorge had grown up in a village in Mexico. Jorge nodded. "Your friend is right. Where I come from, you can't walk like that. You keep your eyes down. You don't go around looking into people's faces, especially police. You must be humble."

Such a thought makes Americans bristle. We are not inclined to go about with downcast eyes, even—maybe especially—in the presence of authority. After all, our national identity took shape in resistance to what many colonials regarded as overreaching authority. The signers of the Declaration of

Independence blamed King George III for the rift between England and America. He had, they said, violated the rights of colonists, and therefore had forfeited their allegiance. Better to die, Patrick Henry thundered, than to submit to despotic power.

One of the colonial navy's battle flags dramatically indicated American defiance of imperial authority: a snake coiled, ready to strike, and the legend, "Don't Tread on Me." And when England finally decided that the war in America was too expensive and perhaps unwinnable, and recognized American independence, the Americans designed a government, described in The Articles of Confederation, that was so weak it was hardly a national government at all. This arrangement was replaced by the Constitution of the United States, which provided for a stronger central government, but had "checks and balances" designed to make sure that none of the three branches of government could accumulate too much power.

I make the point again: every American-born citizen has grown up in a society that has distrust of authority at its political core.

I once spent a summer in England as the guest of a former student. I stayed in an apartment above her boathouse on the Thames. One afternoon as we sat with a group of her friends, one of them asked about the differences I might have found between Americans and Brits.

"Well," I said, "you seem comfortable with a level of regulation that Americans would not tolerate." I had in mind, for example, that English homeowners had to get permission from some sort of bureau to replace a roof. And if the old roof were thatch, the new roof would be too, no matter how expensive it might be.

Eyebrows around the table went up as much as polite Brits would allow. "What do you mean?"

I explained that in America people wouldn't like being told what sort of roof they could have, or what tree on their property could or could not be cut, and in fact disliked what they regarded as any governmental interference in their lives at all.

"Well, how do you get things done, then?" my new friends wanted to know.

"We generally think we can do a better job ourselves than if government gets involved," I explained.

The conversation wobbled to a halt and limped off in another direction. Clearly these good English citizens didn't know what to say in the face of such outrageous nonsense, and I didn't know how to make myself any plainer. I had never felt more American.

I'm not suggesting that we Americans are wrong in our emphasis on the rights and freedoms of the individual and our suspicion of governmental power. Such suspicion is well founded. But—speaking for myself, at least—American deep-rooted distrust of authority has led to some confusion about our relationship to a God Whose authority is absolute. He is not, after all, a popularly elected president; He is King of Kings and Lord of Lords. His word is law, and while His commandments "are not grievous," neither are they negotiable.

And if our cultural and political heritage makes us bridle at the thought of being subjects, we positively rebel at the thought of being servants. Yet Paul spoke of being a bond servant of Jesus Christ (Romans 1:1). Jude called himself a servant of Jesus (verse 1), and it's clear that he did not mean a hired hand who could quit if he felt like it.

Given our national experience—our national shame—with race-based slavery, it's difficult for us to get past the language. Our racial history has at its center the story of the exploitation of people based on the color of their skin and the hopeless condition into which tens of thousands of victims were born or forced by criminal activity. We immediately think of people systematically degraded physically, economically, and emotionally, people whose humanity was denied in order that they might be bought, sold, and used like mules or oxen.

Reading Paul's words, I used to wonder why God would want to degrade me like that. How could that metaphor—the bond slave—be reconciled with the metaphor of a son, an heir? My reading was, of course, colored by my culture. Then one day Shakespeare enlightened me.

In Act II, scene 2 of *King Lear*, the Earl of Kent, a man loyal to Lear, has come to the castle of the Duke of Cornwall. With his wife, who is Lear's daughter Regan, Cornwall is on the verge of revolt against the aged king. The meeting does not go well and the angry Cornwall orders, "Fetch forth the stocks!" Kent's reply is instructive: "Call not your stocks for me. I serve the king, on whose employment I was sent to you."

Here's what I took from that. Kent, a man of no mean status himself, willingly, gladly, set aside his own cares and welfare to serve one greater than himself. In another time and another place, another culture, everyone watching the play understood that this was right.

Even more to the point, noble Kent was not diminished in this. Quite the opposite: when he was opposed and threatened, he answered not out of a claim of his own status, which was, after all, no greater than that of the rebel Cornwall, but out of a claim of the power and status of the king, "on whose employment I was sent to you." Cornwall's offense, then, was not so much against Kent as against the king himself.

Alistair Cooke, the astute British journalist who for many years lived in America, once succinctly observed that the U.S. Constitution has one central meaning: no kings.

Bull's-eye.

But perhaps our nation's birth—a throwing off of the authority of a flawed earthly king—and our association of servanthood with degradation and dishonor has blinded us to the dignity and power of being a servant of the Most High.

Our "reasonable service," representing the King of Kings, endows our lives with beauty, grace, and authority. And one more thing: At the end of our earthly service we can expect to hear, "Well done, good and faithful servant. Enter into the joy of thy Lord."

What better way to live?

The Catalog of Kitsch
1990

For a hundred dollars I could buy a pen that writes upside down and under water. Or a remote-controlled metalized Mylar 52" blimp, "the perfect size," the airline catalog pointed out, "for hovering around your home in eerie near silence." Or for the same hundred dollar bill I could acquire an eleven-inch-high waterfall lamp which also dispenses the "soothing aroma of violet-scented oil (included)," and get a dollar in change.

For two hundred bucks I could order The Total Gym: "Feel Terrific with the Body You've Always Desired." And if my workout left me feeling not so terrific, I could get relief for a mere nineteen dollars by replacing the strap on my shoulder bag with a "patented magnet strap" which would offer the benefits of "12 therapeutic, bi-polar mini magnets sewn invisibly into the light padding."

There was a bubble machine, to improve my parties, gold-plated brass collar stays, end tables in the shapes of zebras and giraffes, and, for $125, a cartoon moose standing on his hind legs, fore hooves casually crossed on his chest, his antlers supporting a round glass top.

What kind of greed and cynicism, I wondered, must be behind the manufacture and marketing of such rubbish? Did these peddlers actually believe that there were people so wealthy, bored and destitute of taste that they would burden their credit cards and clutter their homes with these objects?

Apparently so. And apparently when we have more money than is actually useful, when we have bought everything we need and our lust for acquisition is still unsated, we will buy things that are useless— worse than useless, things that are ugly and ridiculous and a shame to a civilization so anesthetized by its own casual wealth it can't think what to do with it all.

One of my students is preparing for a mission trip to Mongolia, which, he reports, is experiencing a "dzud," a drought so severe and so protracted that up to a fifth of the population, herders in remote areas, may well watch their livestock die, then their children. The Mongolian government has asked for eight million dollars in aid, less, I'm guessing, than the market value of the shiny junk crowding the pages of the airline catalog, far less than the fifteen to twenty million scooped up in a week by a successful film debut.

The catalog, the student essay, these had been part of my reading in the several days before I saw the church. I was walking down a wide, moneyed boulevard in a wealthy city, and there it was, enormous and white, wedding cake white, white and sleek as the gleaming yachts just a few blocks away, white as the clouds in the sunny blue sky, and for many Americans and most of the world, surely as remote.

A bright fountain splashed and winked. A stretch limo, gleaming white except for its darkened windows, nosed along the curling driveway.

I couldn't say exactly why the place made me feel uneasy, embarrassed, even ashamed. By reputation this was one of the model mega-churches of evangelical America, and I have no doubt that many good and praiseworthy things happen there.

It's not that I'm averse to big churches, either. During a summer's stay in England I found that the great old churches, chapels and cathedrals prompted me to prayer and contemplation as few other things have.

So why was this different? Why didn't I want to pray here? Why did I feel relieved to turn the corner and put this place behind me? After all, it emanated American success. Ted Turner said that life is a game, and money is what you keep score with. This place must be teeming with winners.

And maybe that was the problem.

I thought of my youngest brother's sudden ascent, years ago, to athletic stardom. In one amazing season he transformed himself from nameless sub to scoring phenomenon, briefly and locally famous as high school sports heroes are. Along with the name recognition and the all-conference selection came a scholarship offer to attend a well-known and expensive Christian camp. He had become valuable, a handsome and suddenly popular demonstration that Christianity is not for losers.

But it is. It is for thieves and beggars and lepers. It is for the once proud rabbi on the road to Damascus who, in a brief thunderclap, sees that he must lose it all—the reputation, the ascending career, the powerful friends, all the shiny junk in the catalog of success.

It is for all those who have confronted their own poverty of spirit, who have taken a good look in the mirror and found dirty mouths, dirty hands and clothes that are just ill-fitting rags. Who see that they are not pretty. And who know that's just about the best they can do.

Losers.

My church has been investing heavily in a remodeling project: new carpet, big new screen to display the pastel lettering generated by the computer, heavy-duty sound system. Maybe all this is a good idea, maybe it's just expensive junk; I'm not sure. I'll leave that to the church leaders to figure out.

I do know this. I have to keep my own house, the house of the soul, free of the gaudy trash too easily acquired, the cheap kitsch of the spirit all too readily available. I must keep close company with One who had no place to lay His head, of Whom it had been said "there was no beauty that we should desire Him." Who made Himself "of no reputation," and invites me to imitate Him.

Who presents me with the paradox of losing my life to find it.

This may not play well in the American market place. Its only virtue is that it's liberating and transforming in the way that truth always is.

Radical Subjectivity

Spring 2009

My older daughter is pursuing a degree at the local extension of one of our state universities. Not surprisingly, the course offerings are more limited than at the main campus, and since she is pursuing a career in social work, she signed up for one of the required courses in Women's Studies.

Women's Studies is a relatively recent and notoriously doctrinaire addition to university departments, and I had warned my daughter about what she was likely to encounter: the most shrill, angry, and even irrational fringes of the feminist movement. Indeed, some of the more extreme apologists for Women's Studies have claimed that rationality is a male way of thinking and should not be imposed on females.

Still, we were both taken aback at the unbending and unapologetic polemics of the course, which turned out to be primarily a barrage of propaganda in support of all manner of nonheterosexual identities and behaviors: gay, lesbian, and transsexual (those who through surgery and hormone treatments have tried to alter their gender).

There was little of what would normally be called scholarship, and, in any event, scholarship—the discovery, examination, synthesis, and application of information—was not the aim of the course. The aim was the propagation of a set of attitudes about the subject, and the acceptable set was not simply tolerance, but approval and advocacy.

It was a course that violated everything universities claim about themselves: places where truth is pursued and disseminated objectively and fairly, and where differences of opinion are welcomed as part of this pursuit. Instead, dissent was bullied into silence and probing questions were shuffled off as inappropriate to the course's aim—as, of course, they were. Small wonder, then, that my daughter came to refer to this course as an encounter with the Lesbian Gestapo.

What caught my special attention was the glossary of terms that were central to the course's vocabulary, this one in particular: "Sex: an identity assigned at birth by doctors, parents, and others." Here, clear and dramatic, was the central issue dividing a Christian mind, a Christian understanding of truth, from what has come to be called postmodernism. Here was an example of the watershed issue of thinking and understanding in the first decade of the 21st century. Here we are confronting what I'll call radical subjectivity.

The question is this: Is truth external and independent of our own minds, or is truth contingent and variable, simply a social, political and psychological construct?

If the first is true, if truth is objective, then we must conform our understanding and our behavior to its contours. Scripture puts it this way: "This is the way; walk in it." The task of a Christian thinker, then, is to learn what is true—that is to say, to discover some part of the mind of God—and conform our understanding and our behavior to that truth.

Sometimes this is physical truth, and only lunatics would try to ignore the facts of physics. If the lift force of an airplane's wings is inadequate to overcome the plane's weight—because of overloading, say—then the plane won't fly. This fact is not contingent on my understanding or wishes or on the experiences that shaped my psychological outlook. It just *is*, and to ignore it is to ensure disaster.

It matters not at all if the plane's designers and pilot are Christians. It's not "their" physics. It works the same for everybody, and all designers and pilots had better understand what is required to get the plane in the air and keep it there. This is not an *assigned* understanding; it's a *recognition* of what is and how things work.

Christians insist there is also what I'll call a moral universe, whose laws are, like the laws of physics, both discoverable and binding.

It's not only Christians who believe this. In the Declaration of Independence, Thomas Jefferson appealed to the "laws of nature and of nature's God." And when another son of the Enlightenment, Ben Franklin, set out in pursuit of moral perfection, he made a chart of thirteen virtues, such as chastity and temperance, and measured his daily behavior against this standard.

Of course Franklin never achieved anything like moral perfection, but the point here is that he recognized a universally authoritative, objective standard of right behavior. To be morally responsible required him to measure his conduct against that standard. The blots Franklin entered on the chart marked his recognition that he had often been "found wanting," that he had not measured up. This standard was not "his morality," as the contemporary phrase would have it, but existed independently and was binding upon everyone.

So what lies behind the astonishing definition of sex that my daughter encountered in her classroom? The answer is a denial of the most obvious implications of a biological fact, that to be born with male sex organs means one is a male, and to be born with female reproductive organs means one is a female.

One would think this is obvious: The doctor holds up a newly delivered infant, takes a look at the plumbing, and announces, "It's a boy." It's really not hard to tell; after all, generation after generation has been able to tell, and in precisely the same way: they looked at what was there. And, contrary to what my daughter's instructor claimed, this sexual identity is not *assigned*; it's *recognized*.

And from this recognition certain behavioral expectations follow. Male and female organs, whether belonging to roosters and hens, stags and does, or men and women, are complementary. They have their purposes, and we understand what those purposes are, just as we understand that the forms of our molars or our ears or our nostrils indicate their functions.

But none of this matters to the radical subjectivists. Biological facts don't determine gender identification; what matters is how they feel. If an anatomical male says he feels like a girl, well, it's up to him to decide which he is.

And if anatomy is not recognized as determiners of sex, it's hardly surprising that many postmodern thinkers reject the idea of objective moral standards. In other words, if sexual identity is not a matter of easily observed objective biological markers, but is instead a matter of how one feels—if sexual identification is unmoored from sexual facts—then it's easy to reject the idea of objective moral markers. My conduct will be guided and judged not by referencing a standard outside my own preferences and inclinations, a standard that includes virtues such as chastity and temperance, but by—well, by referencing what? Anything at all?

If there is no external referent for our conduct, then how can we tell if we're doing the right thing? If, as so many now insist, what used to be understood as moral statements—"thou shalts" and "thou shalt nots"—are merely statements of power (if, for example, objections to abortion are only the rhetoric of those trying to maintain the subjugation of women), then by what standard is behavior to be judged?

In other words, when people insist that "morality can't be legislated," and "you can't impose *your* morality on *me*," they are disclaiming any common moral authority, an authority outside merely individual preferences; so how can anyone judge what is right conduct?

And here, of course, the postmodern ethicist has run himself into a cul-de-sac, for he cannot live in a world devoid of objective moral standards. He won't talk long without making value statements that he believes to be morally binding on everyone. When, for example, he declares that a ban on abortion is unfair to women, he has just abandoned his claim that there are no universal moral absolutes. He is saying that we all have the idea that people should be treated fairly. He is adamant about this. He would be shocked if someone replied, "Well, who cares about fairness? That's your morality, and you should not try to impose it on anyone else."

There are plenty of arguments about what "fair" means.

Is it fair to try to treat every child in the family

exactly the same, or does fair treatment take into account differences in age, temperament, and talents? Is it fair that Bill Gates must pay taxes at a higher rate than I do to use the same interstate highway and be protected by the same military forces? Is it fair that a genetically gifted athlete earns millions playing games while a hard-working field hand gets little more than minimum wage for producing our food?

Here's the point: We can argue about the *application* of a moral truth, but only because we recognize that moral truth, that fact in the moral universe. Otherwise, we are simply reporting feelings and preferences.

Christians must take care to keep in mind Scriptural bases for making judgments. I am uneasy when my students tell me that the day's chapel was a "good" one because they had "felt really blessed." I'm glad they felt good, but all too often, I'm afraid, they really mean they were excited. It would be just as easy to say, as some might have said, that it was a "bad" chapel because it didn't excite them. The referent for judgment is their own feelings and little else.

Men and women walk away from marriages, abandoning sacred vows and damaging their children's sense of security, for the same reason. They believe something else—or someone else—will produce better feelings, and that is the standard of moral measurement. Good people leave good churches because, they claim, their needs are not being met.

Feelings matter. But they cannot be the standard driving our conduct. Devoted soldiers do their duty even when—especially when—they are tired and hungry and frightened. Responsible adults go to work when they'd rather snooze or golf or fish. Good parents care for their children every day, including days when the kids are cranky, disrespectful, and generally unpleasant to be around.

In an age when we hear daily that truth depends, that truth is contingent, Christians must remember that we live in the kingdom of the great I Am, the One Who embodies eternal truth. It is His righteousness, not our own, that we must seek, embrace, and live out.

Biblical Economics

May 2010

From here you wouldn't know the U. S. economy is, depending on the expert, either on the verge of a recession or already in one. My wife and I are in Southern California for a week's vacation. Part of the time we'll spend with old friends, sharing their home and enjoying their company. We'll eat together, catch a game at Dodger Stadium, and take a day trip to Catalina Island, twenty-six miles across the sea, as the old song goes.

But Bonnie and I needed some time alone, too, and here we are in a hotel at Marina Del Rey, the small-boat harbor of Los Angeles. We shopped around on the internet, found a place we could afford for a few days, and when we arrived were pleased to hear that we had been given an upgrade to a room overlooking the water and probably five hundred boats. Some of them are modest as these things go, others are astonishing in size and opulence. One is easily as long as my house, and I count eleven antennas sprouting from the bridge, indicating an array of electronic gear worth more than my house.

The sun slips into the Pacific, the lilac-colored water darkening as the sunset fades, and in several boats cabin lights come on. The rest are dark, indicating the willingness of owners to pay whopping dockage fees so they can enjoy their boats on weekends. We're not far from LAX, and I count, bright pearls against the dark sky, the landing lights of big jets on a descending flight path: five, six, eight, nine. The city seems as busy as ever, and in the part of it that I can see—and I can see only one part of the huge marina—money flows like water. There are hundreds of luxury condos, and scores more under construction. I look out over the forest of masts at the lights of these places and wonder who these people are and how they acquired so much money.

There seems to be a weight of wealth here that's as immovable as a mountain.

But history and the evening news tell a different story. Once the palaces of Babylon were drenched with the wealth of the Fertile Crescent. Once the streets of Rome celebrated Roman conquests by cheering the generals and their parades of treasures, wagonloads of it, looted from the conquered. Once Montezuma's capital had so much gold that the Aztecs filled a room with it, ransom for their king whom the Spaniards killed anyway.

And now Babylon is desert, the great Forum a ruin, the Aztec civilization destroyed.

Here at the great marina it's hard to imagine anything that could bring this kind of wealth and power to its knees.

And yet...airlines are cutting back on routes, eliminating meals, even going out of business. Thousands of families unable to make payments on homes purchased with risky loans are giving their keys to their banks and walking away. The nation's trade deficit and national debt are increasing at disturbing rates. The American dollar continues to lose value against the euro and the pound. On my last visit to Canada several years ago the greenback was worth $1.35 Canadian. Now the exchange is at par.

Some of these economic problems seem to be the consequences of poor judgment and are amenable to correction. Others, economists say, result from expanding economies and cheap labor in China and India, countries whose increasing demand for oil is also partially responsible for increases in fuel prices in America, increases reflected in higher prices for goods and food. Still other economic woes likely reflect the cycles of expansion and contraction characteristic of capitalist economies.

A recent news item reports an increasing number of Americans raiding their retirement accounts to make mortgage payments. If these folks are counting on Social Security to fully support them in retirement, some financial advisors say, they may be in for an unpleasant surprise.

Does the Bible have anything to say about this? Surely. It doesn't tell us how to manage a portfolio or whether hydrogen is the smart energy of the future. More importantly, it puts economic concerns in perspective.

It tells us, first of all, that money is not to be our chief concern. The writer of Ecclesiastes noted that those who love wealth will never be satisfied, no matter how much they have (Ecclesiastes 5:10), and Paul reminds Timothy that the love of money is a root for all kinds of evil (1 Timothy 6:10).

As Saul of Tarsus, Paul apparently grew up in a prosperous family. He offers a model perspective when he reports that he has had plenty and has suffered need (think of him in a Roman jail asking a friend to bring him books and his warm coat before winter arrives), and has learned in both circumstances to be content.

Finally, let's remember that Jesus assured us that our heavenly Father knows that we need food, clothing, and shelter. The One who clothes the wildflowers will clothe His children.

He doesn't promise cruises or Cadillacs. It may be that we have mistakenly come to regard a luxurious standard of living as some kind of birthright. Now may be the time to learn to live happily with less.

My own perspective was adjusted several years ago when a man working on a crew laying foundations for a neighboring property asked about "the little house," and pointed to my back yard. It turned out that "the little house" was my tool shed. His English wasn't much better than my Spanish, but I finally realized that he was asking about living in it.

I took him into the back yard, opened the shed door, and gestured toward my mower and rakes and shovels. No lighting, no plumbing, not even a window. "See?" I said. "It's just a tool shed. You can't live there."

"I can," he said, "I pay you rent."

I tried to explain that letting him sleep there would be against the law. I don't think he understood.

I didn't even try to explain that I was not the rich man he thought I was. He could see my two cars. They were each a decade and more old, but they ran well. He could see my green backyard, and the grapevines and tomatoes, and the daylilies and hydrangeas in bloom. He could see that my house had enough space for bedrooms for every member of the family. I was a rich American, no?

Well...well, yes. I have more than enough shoes and shirts and space and food. Probably too much food.

I don't have a yacht or even a modest sailboat. I do have a canoe that provides a restful and pleasant float on the steams of the beautiful valley where I live.

And I'm reminded that all I see now—the wealth of a great city spread out before me—is as temporary as the shine on a soap bubble. My own inheritance is in heaven, a treasure unaffected by a weakening currency, a shaky stock market and rising energy costs.

Am I rich, then? Beyond imagining.

Wearing the Yellow Jersey

March 2014

In May of 2013 Nike made it official. They were done with Lance Armstrong and the charity that bore his name—once proudly, but no longer. By now, all those yellow "Live Strong" bracelets so popular a few years ago have probably gone to the dump, along with Lance Armstrong's reputation.

Not so long ago it seemed that Armstrong had it all. He had not only overcome cancer, but had become one of the greatest athletes of his generation, winning the most prestigious of all professional cycling races, the Tour de France, an astonishing seven times. He was famous, rich—reportedly worth around $100,000,000 (count the zeros; that's a hundred million bucks, friends)—handsome, and, for a while, was engaged to Sheryl Crow, the beautiful and talented musician.

He raised millions for the charity that bore his name, Lance Armstrong. This guy even had a perfect name for a macho superstar American athlete. Lance.

Armstrong. Had his parents been prophets?

He was held up to young athletes as a model competitor. And no wonder. This was a man who, on world television, pedaled up next to his chief competitor on a long, hot mountain climb, looked over at the guy, caught his eye, gave him a long stare, and then sped off, crushing any hope that anybody but Lance would wear the winner's yellow jersey that year. There were several stages left in the race, but the contest was over. Armstrong knew it, the other riders knew it, millions watching the race knew it. It was a remarkable athletic moment: supreme confidence wedded to supreme achievement.

His feats of strength and endurance seemed beyond the bounds of human athletic possibility.

And apparently they were. Suspicion grew to rumor, rumor to accusation, accusation to denial. The great champion insisted that he had never used PEDs, performance-enhancing drugs. He threatened to sue people and publications that continued to suggest that he had juiced, and one such publication actually forked over $600,000 to the offended rider, who pointed out that he had never failed a drug test.

That part was true. In fact, he had learned how to mask the drugs and fool the test.

But finally there was just too much evidence for Armstrong to plausibly deny. Eyewitnesses, including some of his own teammates, told a consistent story of what they had seen. The final investigation by the sport's governing body resulted in a document thick as the first draft of a Russian novel.

Armstrong could not continue insisting that he was an innocent victim of others' envy and unfounded suspicion. He was stripped of his championships and banned from competition. He finally agreed to a long interview with Oprah Winfrey, and admitted that he doped and then lied about it, loudly and repeatedly. The hero has been revealed to be a cheat, a liar, and a blustering bully.

So what are we to make of this sorry story? Is this something like an ancient Greek drama, the hero, like Oedipus, brought into the dust, exiled and disgraced as a consequence of pride and unchecked ambition?

Well, yes, I'd say so. There's a reason why these archetypes keep appearing and reappearing in literature and the newspaper: Human beings keep behaving this way—athletes and actors, scholars and singers, presidents and preachers.

Few ministries have been wrecked because a

famous preacher or television evangelist has renounced his theology. But we don't have to initiate a Google search to begin to count those brought down by the perils of power, fame, and wealth, and the distorted egos that too often ensue.

Some years ago I received a flyer in the mail asking me to be on the lookout for singing talent, since the son of a well-known TV evangelist and talk-show host was, in imitation of "Star Search" and "American Idol," launching a program to discover Christian stars.

I thought then—and I think now—that that was one of the worst ideas I had ever heard. Exactly how, I wondered, does that adjective, *Christian*, go with that noun, *star*?

Well, it doesn't. And it can't. The trappings of stardom not only deflect us from the example of Christ, who taught us to kneel and wash one another's feet, but place us in great danger. Experience tells us that the rich and idolized often behave badly. For many of these folks there's too much power and not enough restraint. They can pretty much do what they want to do, and too many behave like spoiled children. We would like to believe that, given great wealth, fame, and adulation, we would do better.

But we probably wouldn't. I can't think of a

single reason to believe that I would.

Don't misunderstand me. I'm not arguing for failure. I'm not a teacher so I can help my students prepare to fail. And I don't think there's any inherent virtue in poverty. Poor people often behave badly too.

But I am asking us all to think carefully about how we define and measure success in our lives and in our churches. About whether we want to spend our lives pursuing the values advanced by Hollywood and Wall Street, even if—especially if—those values are given a religious paint job, or by those ordered in Scripture and exemplified by Christ Himself. One set leads to trouble; the other, to heaven and a reward for a race fairly won.

In the end, that reward will not be based on many of the ways we often measure success—name recognition, growth in numbers, robust church budgets, desirable as those may be—but on whether we have run patiently and faithfully. Solomon built a great and splendid temple; Jeremiah, for his obedience to the Lord, was denounced and imprisoned in a boggy pit where he nearly suffocated.

Both were obedient to their calling, both diligent in the work God gave them, both winners in the only race that matters for eternity.

Sometimes You Just Gotta Laugh

The Next Step

It's apparent by now that the nation has survived its latest crisis. I'm referring, of course, to Christmas, that threat to civil liberties spied out by the Self-Appointed Thought Police who discern in the C-Word what you and I, dear reader, never had: an assault on the consciences of innocent citizens and a threat to civil liberties everywhere. Until recently nobody understood how subversive "tidings of comfort and joy" could be.

My consciousness was raised several years ago when a high official in the local school district was quoted in the local paper as saying that teachers were admonished to avoid saying "Christmas." That was the same year that the city manager of Eugene [Oregon] told city firefighters they could no longer put up a Christmas tree in the fire station. It seemed that some new watershed had been discovered by the explorers of social sensitivity, a sort of continental divide of correctness unmapped until then.

I was recently reminded of the good services of these folks when my granddaughter brought home from school a memo on the dates of "Winter Break." It turns out that this break was scheduled not at the end of the term, as one might expect, but right around December 25, the date marked in red on my calendar by some politically uninstructed publishers as, well, you know.

And there were all those offensive lights, all that gift giving, and old Bing Crosby, that historic political desperado, claiming it was C-s time in the city.

In spite of these dangerous behaviors, it turns out that we have escaped the establishment of anything like a Church of the United States, a national church supported by taxes and coercing consciences, the very thing the framers of the Constitution wanted to avoid. No up-to-date Scrooges have been arrested and indicted for Bahing and Humbugging. No revenue agents have required a single coin to be turned over to a bell ringer. Bill Maher has not been charged and tried on suspicion of disrespect toward Christianity, no matter how overwhelming the evidence. Perhaps we had a near miss, but it was a clean miss, thank G-d.

Nonetheless, if eternal vigilance is the price of liberty perhaps the SATP have not gone far enough. To begin with, the designation of Winter Holiday may still offend the linguistically astute, "holiday" being derived, as they know, from "holy day."

And all those offensive place names: San Antonio and San Diego and San Francisco, St. Paul and St. Augustine and St. Louis, Corpus Christi and Hollywood, named after a shrub whose red berries are traditionally associated with the blood of Christ. We'll need new names for these cities, and for the American half of the Saint Lawrence River. Officials in Quebec, it seems, offer a dangerously wide latitude in speech as long as it's French. But that's their problem. All we can do for them is offer an up-to-date model of offense-free speech and hope they will follow.

Once Saint Nicholas has been relocated from the North Pole to Siberia we'll be free to make some sensible adjustments to our school calendar, and move Winter Break to the end of the academic semester where it logically belongs. The fall school calendar will benefit from a couple of extra days, too, since Thanksgiving will be eliminated.

(Let's not play games here, folks. Abraham Lincoln's proclamation establishing Thanksgiving makes it all too clear Who should be thanked.)

Halloween is out, too. Some conservative Christians object to its allegedly pagan origins and depictions of witches and vampires.

Labor Day? That's an unfair and insensitive privileging of workers, with no equal celebration of middle management.

Independence Day has to go as well. Have we forgotten its connection to a war? Several years ago some protesters pointed out that the team name of the University of Massachusetts—the Minutemen—was militaristic and sexist, calling up visions of men with muskets. Why didn't we listen?

And think about Cinco de Mayo, a big fiesta celebrating the defeat of a French force by Mexican soldiers. Why do we insist on bringing this up every year? Imagine how the French must feel.

All this has got to stop. Once we have explained the problem to our kids and cleaned up our calendar perhaps we can celebrate with a—umm—Special Day. If nobody minds.

Sometimes You Just Gotta Laugh
1983

Several years ago one of my students offered me some good advice. "Sometimes," said Rose, "sometimes, you just gotta laugh.

I remembered that sage advice last month when all the aging machinery in my house seemed to have entered into some kind of mutual death pact. Almost simultaneously, automobiles, dishwasher, and refrigerator announced serious, even fatal, infirmities.

The guy from JL's Appliance pulled the innards out of the dishwasher, shook his head mournfully and announced that the wheezing, clunking machine would be cheaper to replace than to repair. "It's old," he said. "Find somebody to haul it away."

I'd been wheezing and clunking a bit myself since my recent fifty-first birthday. Just a bit, mind you, but still I found his attitude disquieting. My wife, less sensitive, missed the implications of his remark altogether. She already had a color picked out for the new washer.

Three days later something was wrong with her car. "It's making a really bad sound," she said. "Kind of a clunking, grinding noise."

It was, said the mechanic, the compressor for the air conditioner. Expensive. Well, we wondered, could we drive the car and just leave the air conditioner off?

He gave us the same mournful headshake the dishwasher guy had displayed. "Uh-uh. No way. This belt here also drives your water pump and your power steering. It all runs off—."

"Okay," I said, "give me an estimate."

"Won't know for sure until we get the thing apart," he said, and suggested a minimum that made me suspect that he had once worked for the federal government.

That afternoon he called. "Bearings, shaft, everything's shot in there," he said. "We need to replace the unit." Then he quoted a new price, one which made me certain that he had worked for the government.

Then what I hoped would be a routine brake job on the other car turned out not to be quite so routine. "Calipers are shot," the mechanic explained. "Time to get some new ones. If these old things let go—."

"Sure," I said. "How much?"

"Well, these cars and the Chevy Lumina have

kind of an unusual setup."

"How much?"

He told me. I thought of Rose's admonition.

"What's so funny?" the mechanic asked, taking a step back. I choked down my giggles.

"Oh, uh, look, just go ahead with the work while I call my banker."

The next Tuesday I awoke to find my wife, the resident early riser, standing by the bed, studying me.

"What?" I said, which is a mouthful for me in the morning.

"How long have we had that refrigerator?" she asked. This was not a question I was prepared to answer so soon after sunrise.

Fortunately, she already knew. "Twelve years," she said. "And remember we bought it second-hand from JL's."

I didn't remember, but no matter. She went right ahead. "You know that strange rattling noise it's been making? It's not making it anymore."

I managed a nod. "Good."

"Well, no, maybe not so good. It's not making any noise at all. It must have died in the night. The milk is warm, but I think the eggs were still okay. I cooked them all. I poached two of them, just the way you like. Why are you laughing?"

We laugh because we are created in the image of God, and it's obvious that He has a very large funny bone. Why else would he make spinach good for kids and chocolate bad for everybody? Why else would He invent sex, with all its absurdities and complications? To women, for example, He gave a longing to communicate, while to men He gave a passion for football.

From the first weekend of September to the middle of January this arrangement must prove endlessly amusing to our Creator. Eve says, "You promised we could spend the day together," and Adam, from his recliner says, "I know. I told the fellas I couldn't watch the game with them today. Have a seat. Henderson is just now teeing it up."

"But I want to talk," Eve says.

"Okay," Adam says. "So what's your read on why so many of Henderson's kickoffs have been going out of bounds lately? Gives the other guys too good a field position. Look there, he just did it again. C'mon, Henderson, you're killing us! Any chips in the pantry, Eve? Eve?"

During the off-season the Lord can amuse Himself by tuning in to the owls and the larks that He has joined together in holy matrimony. The larks, given to practical pursuits, like to be up and doing. At dawn, or just before, their eyes snap open like umbrellas in a high wind, and they begin to hum and bustle. They toss aside one chore after another like a riverboat gambler dealing cards—until lunch, when they slow noticeably. By the time the best restaurants are opening for dinner the larks are done, their wings folded, their once shiny eyes dull.

In God's humorous scheme of things larks are married to owls, creatures who draw energy from the pulsing light of distant galaxies and inspiration from the cool, tranquil moon. Owls love late, leisurely dinners, shooting stars, Keats, and, inexplicably, larks.

We know all about this at our house. My own pretty lark loves to be up at first light, hopping about and singing. By seven o'clock she likes to recite the list of things she has already accomplished, while I stare at my razor, trying hard to remember which end is sharp. Soon she is in the kitchen doing something with eggs and singing hymns; I am trying to decide which sock goes on the left foot, and offering up fervent prayers—silent ones, so I don't have to move my lips—that I might get through the next two hours without hurting myself.

After dark, though, the hot glare of day over, I am in fine feather, brimming with energy, confidence and amour. On a night in September, with football season nicely underway, I have directed a highly satisfactory session of evening school, ripped through a ninety-minute workout at the gym, and, driving home through the cool Oregon night, composed in my head the first two quatrains of a love poem.

The lark is in bed, glasses on, an open book in her hands, cute as ever. The scent of Chanel No. 5 is light but persistent in the room. I clear my throat and recite my lines with considerable ardor and intensity. I can't see her eyes behind the glasses, but I imagine they are shining with delight. She hasn't moved a muscle. Spellbound.

The last line hangs in the air like Chanel No. 5, and still she lies motionless. I cross the room, bend down beside her, lift off her glasses, and—

"Oh, hi," she murmurs, one eye opening a bleary quarter inch. "Didn't...hear you...come in. Can...you...turn out...the light?"

Sometimes you just gotta laugh. Laughter is a gift from God. It is good for the body, exercising dozens of muscles and releasing natural pain-killing chemicals. Norman Cousins, in *Anatomy of an Illness,* tells how he treated a rare, incurable and painful disease with daily doses of comedy. His physicians could offer him little relief from pain and insomnia. He found, however, that an hour of laughing at videotapes of old comedy routines eased his pain, relaxed him, allowed him to sleep, and apparently put him on the road to surprising improvement.

And laughter is good for the soul. Laughing at ourselves is an exercise in humility. It restores our perspective. Our own sense of dignity, we realize in laughter, is not crucial to the maintenance of the universe.

"A merry heart doeth good like a medicine," the proverb says. Given our high-pressure, high-speed lives and the psychic and spiritual cuts and bruises we are sure to accumulate, it's a medicine we all need in generous dollops. To translate the ancient Hebrew Rose's way: "Sometimes you just gotta laugh."

Eating In

The setting is the living room of a middle class home. The characters are Jerry and Sandra, married, both in their early forties.

Note on tone: The banter is good-natured, though sometimes competitive in a lighthearted way. These two people like each other.

Jerry enters. He is dressed in a suit and raincoat. He carries an umbrella in one hand, and in the other a bouquet and a shopping bag. He sets down the bag, folds the umbrella, takes off his coat and hangs it up.

Sandra enters opposite.

S: Jerry, you're home early.

J: Yes, I am. Surprised you, didn't I?

S: Yes you did. Is everything okay?

J: Why would you ask that?

S: Well, you hardly ever get home this early. It's not even three o'clock. The kids aren't even home yet.

J: I know. And they won't be for quite a while. Ray has a biology lab to catch up on after school, and Rosie will be staying to do some work in the library. A paper on Romeo and Juliet, she said.

S: Oh. When do we need to pick them up?

J: I gave Ray some food money for the two of them. They'll get some pizza, then stay at school for the basketball game.

S: That should be about nine? If you have work to do this evening I'll pick them up. Otherwise, maybe you would?

J: There's no work tonight, and no otherwise. I drove over to the school and gave Ray my car keys. Came home in a cab. We have six hours, just the two of us, and (he reaches into the shopping bag) some bubbly, and (reaches in again) some bubble bath, and some Belgian chocolates, and...(he pulls out a good-sized gift-wrapped box) a little something special for the special occasion. Go ahead. Open it.

S: (Sandy unwraps the box, lifts out a slinky, brief nightgown. She looks it over carefully.) That's a *little* something, all right. I haven't worn something like this since...

J: Since May 11, 2009. You came along with me to that conference in San Diego, remember?

S: (Chooses a chocolate, bites it in half, and inspects the uneaten half.) Oh, wow. This is sooo delicious. Was that the time I had the unfortunate experience with the big plate of oysters?

J: It was. As I recall, that night you insisted on taking the side of the bed closest to the bathroom. You shouldn't eat things that you can't tell if they're spoiled. But look on the bright side. You had been saying that you wanted to lose ten pounds. You got halfway to your goal in just one night. And I think you probably set multiple world records in the seven-yard dash. I didn't know you still had that kind of speed.

S: I did have quick feet once upon a time, didn't I?

J: Oh, yeah. You remember the first time I saw you—out on the tennis court in high school?

S: Well, I remember in the middle of practice realizing some guy was ogling me.

J: Eyeing you appreciatively, is what you meant to say.

S: I think it must have been just before the city championships in May. A hot afternoon, as I recall.

J: That's it exactly. Your cheeks were pink, your hair was flying, your eyes were lit up with the heat of competition. You looked great.

S: My eyes were lit up like a neon sign saying Go Away, Go Away.

J: Really? Good thing they didn't mean it. (Pause) We used to play together, didn't we? How come we don't anymore?

S: Tennis, you mean? You don't remember? I beat you eleven times in a row. You finally left your racquet at the park where you knew it would be stolen.

J: Oh. Blame the victim. How can you judge someone's motives?

S: I beg your pardon. You're right. There's no way to know for sure, is there? For instance, I have no idea what you could be up to with all this (indicating the flowers, bottles, chocolates and gown).

J: You know, that's the second time this week the question has been raised. I was in the mall Saturday afternoon when that little meringue there caught my eye in the window of Fig Leaf Lingerie. I was walking out with it in this nice box when Rosie and a couple of her friends spotted me. "Dad," she said. "What are you doing in there?" What kind of a question is that, I'd like to know.

S: Kids can't imagine that their parents have a love life. They know where babies come from, of course, but would like to think that they are an exception.

J: Yeah. That's why I told Ray he was dropped down the chimney by a stork. He seemed relieved.

S: Jerry, really. You told our son that? You shouldn't tell children those stories. When did this conversation take place?

J: Last week. Thursday, I think. (Sandy gives him a hard look, finally has to giggle.) Anyway (opening the bottle and pouring into a couple of goblets he also brings out of the bag) happy anniversary, Babe. (They link arms, sip, kiss, kiss again.)

S: Jerry, this is so sweet of you.

J: Well, I forgot last year, and this year I wanted everything to be just right.

S: You did, didn't you? It shows.

J: Happy 21st anniversary, Sandy.

S: Thank you. But—it's not our anniversary.

J: What? Today is (checks his watch) yes, May 19th, right?

S: Right. But our anniversary was last week, the fifteenth. It's always the fifteenth. Has been for twenty-two years.

J: Oh, man, what a dummy. I'm really sorry. I wasn't even home on the, um—the fifteenth.

S: You were in Tokyo, closing that deal you had been working on so hard for the last couple of months.

J: Sandy, I'm really sorry. I guess I was so absorbed in getting that deal finished everything else kind of shifted out of focus. What a blockhead.

S: Be careful how you talk about my husband, mister. He's a great guy. Jerry, I'm so proud of you. Your boss called an hour ago and told me what a great job you did, and how much he appreciated my sacrifice, I think were his words, with all the long hours you have had to put in on this thing. He invited me to go along with you next month to the trade show in—

guess where—San Diego. He said we would have our evenings free, said we should have a good time and the company would pick up the tab. He recommended a seafood place on Mission Bay. But I'm thinking maybe New York steak, medium well.

J: Good idea. San Diego sounds great, doesn't it? Maybe we'll take one of those dinner cruises out to Coronado Island. Nights can be cool out on the water. You'll have to stand close to me to stay warm. Things will go better this time. Maybe that's the secret of a successful marriage: always try again. (pause) I don't much like Tokyo.

S: I know.

J: I don't like long plane rides.

S: Of course you don't.

J: I missed you and the kids.

S: I know. We missed you, too.

J: I love you, Sandy.

S: (resuming her playful tone) As well you should.

J: I was head over heels from the moment I laid eyes on you.

S: At the tennis court. Couldn't take your eyes off me, could you?

J: That's right. You could tell, huh?

S: Of course. From the minute I saw you coming across the parking lot from the gym.

J: But you wanted me to stop ogling and get lost.

S: Sometimes you are a blockhead. Why do you think I was tossing my hair around like that?

J: We men don't have much of a chance, do we?

S: Jerry?

J: What?

S: Shut up and kiss me.

(The first kiss is light. The second one is deeper and longer. She starts to walk backward out of the room, bringing him with her, still kissing. The phone rings. They freeze, deciding. Finally, without breaking apart, she reaches for the phone.)

S: (Breathlessly) Hello, Mother. Yes, I'm fine. Of course I haven't been running, it's raining outside. No, really, I'm perfectly all right. Wonderful, in fact. (She fans her face with her hand, takes a deep breath.) Do I sound better now? Good. You did what? I see. No, that's all right. I've done it myself on gray rainy days; it's easy to forget to turn them off. Where are you? Which Safeway? Okay, we'll bring the jumper cables. Yes, Jerry's here. No, no, he's fine. Yes, I know he works hard. He just—got off work a little early today. We'll be right there. Listen, while you're waiting would you go to the meat section and pick out a couple of New York steaks for me? It's our anniversary, and we're eating in.

Bible Stories

No Scorekeeping

"Lord," Peter asked Jesus one day, "how often shall my brother sin against me, and I forgive him? Up to seven times?" (Matthew 18:21).

To Peter this must have seemed extraordinarily magnanimous. The law of the fathers required three gestures of forgiveness, but Peter had heard Jesus insist that "unless your righteousness exceed that of the scribes and Pharisees ye shall in no wise inherit the kingdom of God." Seven—more than double that legal requirement—no doubt seemed generous enough to win Jesus' approval.

It wasn't. Jesus said to him, "I do not say to you, up to seven times, but up to seventy times seven." In other words, the issue was not the number that Peter proposed. The issue was that he was counting.

Jesus' answer can be summed up in two words: no scorekeeping.

Don't keep track. It's as simple as that. We must forgive a repentant brother every time, not only for his good but for our own.

Scorekeepers are miserable people. They have discovered that life is not always fair, and they can't get over it. They keep a mental list of offenses they believe have been committed against them, and because they are easily offended the list is long. In the rich drama of life they choose to play suffering martyr, as though this grants them a kind of moral superiority.

This is a delusion; scorekeeping has more to do with selfishness and arrogance than with moral sensitivity. In addition, scorekeeping violates Biblical teaching on love, hope and mercy. And ultimately the scorekeeper becomes isolated, rejecting the fullness of joy and God's family, choosing instead to live apart, like Elijah in his cave, nursing his grievances.

Jesus told a story illustrating this. "A certain man," He said, "had two sons." The brief tale is one of the most familiar of Jesus' many stories. The younger of the sons decides life on the farm is boring. He wants the faster life of the big city. He talks his father into giving him an early inheritance, and heads off toward the bright lights, and for a little while he has a high time living it up with new friends and plenty of girls, one long party, with no thought of the future.

He should have been thinking about it. His

money, of course, soon runs out, the local economy is severely depressed, and for the first time in his life Goodtime Charlie has to look for a job. He's familiar with farm work, and finally lands a job as a swineherd, a dirty, smelly job for anyone, and for a Jewish boy unthinkable. For him pigs are not only physically but religiously unclean, and every moment he spends with them he defiles himself. He has become someone he could never have imagined. He has lost his money, his dignity and even his identity.

Finally—and here is a wonderful phrase—"he came to himself." He has been acting crazy, but now begins to see things clearly: his father, his failure, his future. He sees that he has made a complete mess of things, and unless he repents he will die.

From the far country he sets his face toward home, rehearsing, as he limps along, a confession he must make: "Father, I have sinned against heaven and against thee; I am no longer worthy to be called your son."

True. And it must be said. There's no use pretending that the young man's behavior was anything but hurtful, appalling, disgraceful.

But the point of the story is what happens after repentance, confession and apology.

The father's response has been the subject of many sermons. When he sees his son, filthy, ragged, barefoot, repentant, he is filled with compassion. This is no time for "I told you so!" or "Why didn't you listen?" A hard lesson has been learned; nothing need be said but "Welcome home." There had been enough sorrow and anxiety. Now the family is complete again, an occasion to celebrate. Knock off work early. Fire up the barbecue. Tune the guitars. This is a great day.

It would be nice if the story ended here, but it doesn't. There's another character in this story, an older brother, who at first glance may seem to be as dutiful as the younger brother is negligent, as disciplined as the younger brother is wild, as reliable as the younger brother is erratic.

But a longer look reveals a different sort of character, a man corroded by anger and resentment, a bitter man as unappreciative of his good father and as disrespectful of him in his own way as the boy who left home.

A scorekeeper.

Like all scorekeepers he spends a lot of time and energy on righteous indignation. The world is wrong, and he is here to say how. More precisely, he feels that he has been wronged. And given his system of moral bookkeeping there is some basis for his claim that the ledger is out of balance.

"Your son wasted all that money on prostitutes!" he barks at his father. The indictment is true. "And when he comes home you throw a party for him!" True again. "It's not fair!" Probably not.

It's better than fair. This father is merciful and forgiving, like our heavenly Father. For this we must be now and eternally grateful. "Use every man after his deserts," observed Prince Hamlet, "and who shall 'scape whipping?"

Nor are scorekeepers' books as accurate as they imagine. They are a lot more sensitive to others' faults than their own.

Theirs is likely to be the righteousness of the scribes and Pharisees, who had more rules than anyone could keep, but neglected mercy and forgiveness. Theirs was morality by the numbers, morality that "strained out gnats and swallowed camels," a moral code that generally missed the point.

Big brother misses the point spectacularly. He is legally precise, but morally obtuse. At a time when others are rejoicing at the return of the prodigal, the older brother tries to disown him. In the midst of the father's gladness, the older brother brings him new grief. Scorekeepers injure others and then claim themselves wronged.

Ultimately, of course, they injure themselves. By "refusing to go in" they miss the party. While others are laughing and singing and eating roast beef, the scorekeeper sulks outside, alone, gnawing his own liver.

It's a ridiculous choice. What's more, it's forbidden by our heavenly Father, who insists that we must have compassion and mercy on our "fellow servants," "just as I had pity on you" (Matthew 18:33).

We have all been forgiven unpayable debts. It makes no sense, in turn, to nurture grudges against a brother. The moral of the story is clear: throw away the book of grievances. Join the party. Make glad the Father's heart.

Speech Seasoned with Salt

A friend from my high school youth group e-mails me three or four times a month, and I wish he wouldn't. Or rather, I wish he wouldn't send me his kinds of e-mail. Some he composes, but many of the offerings are political opinion columns that he passes along.

I'm not averse to political opinion columns. I read the op-ed page of our local newspaper every day. I've even written a few, both for the paper's print edition and their electronic version.

Nor do I necessarily disagree with the central ideas in the columns my friend passes along. I'm not bashful about identifying myself as politically and socially conservative, tags that probably apply to most of the writers my friend shares with me and other friends.

What bothers me is the tone of these columns: invariably angry, even shrill, disrespectful, sometimes bordering on malicious and sometimes crossing the border.

I wonder about the purpose of these eruptions.

Can they be meant to convince anyone? If so, they are not likely to succeed. Are we ever convinced because someone shouts at us?

I learned my own lesson on this some years ago. A man had been fired from his job at a local manufacturing firm. He spent several days drinking and brooding, stoking the fires of resentment and rage. Finally he loaded his deer rifle, drove to the plant in search of the man who had sacked him, barged into the lobby, fired a round into the soft drink machine, and when a security guard rushed into the room shot him, too, right though the chest.

There was no doubt about what had happened. There were witnesses. At the shooter's trial his lawyer could do nothing but offer a ridiculous defense: the man would not have behaved this way if he had been sober. "Diminished capacity" was the explanation for the homicide, something like temporary insanity. Yes, he had loaded the gun, driven to the building and shot the guard, but he was not entirely responsible. Some of the blame rested on Demon Rum.

I had been following the trial in the paper, and I thought, "Wow, the defense is desperate. Nobody will buy that explanation."

I was wrong. Twelve people here in Salem,

Oregon, bought it. The murderer was convicted only of a much lesser charge and was sentenced to just a few years in prison.

I was outraged—a state of mind that bestows a wonderful sense of moral superiority, often at the expense of good judgment—and dashed off a guest editorial brimming with sarcasm and contempt for a jury of dunces chosen from a society that all too often shrinks from making appropriate moral judgments.

I pretended to lament my error in teaching my children that people are responsible for their actions, and then closed with what I thought was a flash of brilliant sarcasm that would provide the final smack down of the dopey jurors and any other misguided citizens who might sympathize with the shooter and the verdict. I see now, I said, that I should have been telling my kids that "if you plan to shoot anyone, make sure you and the gun are both loaded."

The newspaper rejected the piece without comment. My guess is that the editor of the op-ed page had the same reaction as one of my friends who read my final draft: "That's not an essay; that's a shout."

Well, umm, yeah, maybe so. And no good came of it.

And what good can come from the kind of

irresponsible and overheated rhetoric that is the currency of so many blogs, so many talk shows and so much political discourse?

The good guys, wearing the colors of the left or the right, have "plans" or "outlines" or "policies"; the bad guys have "schemes." The good guys form alliances; the bad "make deals." People who are concerned about the condition of the environment are dismissed as "tree huggers." Folks who oppose same-sex marriage are "haters" who have a "phobia."

Don Imus, a notorious "shock jock," seemed genuinely surprised when an on-the-air racial insult finally got him fired. After all, hadn't he become rich and famous by peppering his morning program with crude comments?

All this is to say that American discourse, both public and private, has all too often become crude, angry, aggressive, and malicious.

Most colleges and universities include student responses as part of professors' and courses' evaluations. Some years ago Corban University, where I teach, decided to make electronic responses part of the process. The results were startling: a significant number of anonymous student comments were harsh, personal and flippant. One of my colleagues, a good teacher who had always received high ratings from students, was so upset by some of the remarks directed at her that she became ill.

I doubt that she had suddenly forgotten how to teach. I suspect, rather, that students who spent too much time in chat rooms where "flaming"—aggressive, hostile, and insulting speech—is common felt free to flame a skilled and caring teacher.

Whatever the reasons for the kind of speech we're talking about, Christians should have no part of it.

Our speech is to be marked by grace, "seasoned with salt," Scripture says. To mix a metaphor, it should taste good to the ear.

This is not to say that Christians should be less than firm in speaking the truth. And when we speak firmly some people will be angry. We can't help that. But we must make sure that the offense is with the Gospel, not with our own abrasive speech or truculent demeanor.

Perhaps Daniel offers a pattern for us. Working in the court of a pagan emperor who was no friend of God, Daniel lived a life steadfast in faith, but constant in respect and service to the emperor. And when Daniel was forced by a godly conscience to disobey an imperial decree the emperor himself, though compelled by law to impose a severe sentence, was compelled by conscience to affirm Daniel's character and even to praise Daniel's God.

A good outcome, and a good pattern for us all.

A Better Way

The young man's heart must have been pounding like a hammer in a Roman shipyard. The next ten minutes would tell whether he would be branded on the forehead, beaten, hauled to a slave market, or maybe even sold into the quarries, a common fate for Roman criminals. There he would be worked without respite from sunrise until dusk, seven days a week, until killed by accident or by disease brought on by rock dust, malnutrition, and exhaustion.

And a criminal he was, no doubt about it. He had absconded from his master, which was tantamount to grand theft in a slave economy, and apparently took some of his owner's cash with him. He had been gone for months, traveling nearly a thousand miles from his master's home in the eastern provinces to lose himself among the great throngs of Rome.

Now he was back—not in custody, but voluntarily—accompanied by a friend, Tychicus, with nothing between himself and the quarries but a letter.

We can only imagine the state of mind of his

master—Philemon was this master's name, a successful businessman of Colossae—as he stared at the young man, took the letter, and cracked open the seal. "Paul," he read, "a prisoner of Jesus Christ, and Timothy our brother, unto Philemon our dearly beloved, and fellow labourer...grace to you, and peace..."

An old friend of Philemon's was writing him from Rome, where he was in custody awaiting a hearing with the emperor. The charges against this friend—sedition and profanation of the Jewish temple in Jerusalem—were clearly bogus. Two Roman governors had heard the case and knew Paul had broken no laws. But rather than go through another trial, this time in Jerusalem, where a band of would-be assassins had sworn to kill him, Paul had exercised his rights as a Roman citizen and appealed his case to Caesar.

We don't know how the apostle and the runaway slave encountered one another in Rome. Perhaps, like the Prodigal Son, Onesimus had run through his money, learned Paul's whereabouts, and had come to the apostle humbled and penitent. Perhaps his conscience had been keeping him awake. Perhaps Mark, or Aristarchus, or Demas, or Luke were, with

Paul, friends of Philemon and encountered Onesimus in the Roman marketplace.

Somehow, no matter how exactly, the runaway thief and his master's old friend had found one another in the big city. They had come a long way to meet here—one from Jerusalem by way of Caesarea, the other dodging the law all the way from Colossae. An amazing coincidence, some might say. I'm sure Paul and Onesimus would say differently.

An ironic name, Onesimus. It meant "profitable," but the slave with that name had been anything but profitable. We can be sure that running off with a purse full of Philemon's money was not the first time Onesimus had been a problem. It was not unusual for slaves to do all they could to shirk their duties and outwit their masters. Plautus, the Roman comic dramatist, had made the wily, dishonest slave a stock character in his plays, and Paul in a number of his letters admonishes slaves who had become Christians to work hard and honestly for their masters, an indication that some of them, at least, had not always done so.

What was this, then, that Philemon was reading? "I beseech thee for my son Onesimus, whom I have begotten in my bonds: Which in time past was to thee unprofitable"—a pun with a painful truth, Philemon may have thought—"but now profitable to thee and to me: Whom I have sent again: thou therefore receive him…"

Philemon apparently could recognize Paul's handwriting. They had been friends for some time. Here, now, was a test of that friendship. Paul was asking Philemon to take into his home a man who had robbed him. Had the old man lost his mind? Had he been conned by a clever crook?

Not at all. Paul knew better than anyone that people who are in Christ are not who they were without Him. Paul himself, after all, had once been a killer of Christians. That was when he had been known by the name Saul of Tarsus, so driven by misguided zeal that he gave himself over to ferreting out these people of the Way and making sure they ended up in prison—or the grave.

Until one day on the road to Damascus when everything changed—his understanding, his mission, even his name. The Jesus whom Paul had hated and persecuted became his Savior and Lord.

But who would believe that? Ananias, a Christian in Damascus, had needed to hear the voice of God before he would believe it. And later, when Paul went to Jerusalem, and "assayed to join himself to the disciples...they were all afraid of him, and believed not that he was a disciple" (Acts 9:26).

And then something wonderful happened. One of the most influential Christians in Jerusalem, Barnabas, Son of Encouragement, spoke up for him.

And now, years later, Paul the apostle was speaking up for Onesimus: "Receive him...not now as a servant, but above a servant, a brother beloved... receive him as myself."

There was risk here, plenty of it for everyone. Onesimus had no guarantee that Philemon would do as Paul asked. Paul was risking a friendship; if Philemon took Onesimus back on the terms Paul outlined and Onesimus became a problem again, Paul would be partly responsible.

Philemon had risks to consider even if Onesimus would prove to be the changed man Paul said he was. If Onesimus went unpunished, what effect might this lapse in control over a slave have on Philemon's other slaves? And his wealthy friends and business associates might be very unhappy if a runaway, thieving slave were allowed to return without consequences. What ideas might that put into the heads of their servants?

It turned out the risks were worth taking. Paul, after all, was not rash and hasty in judgment. Onesimus had proven himself to be a reliable worker, a help and comfort to the imprisoned apostle. Philemon had every reason to trust Paul's affirmation of Onesimus.

And while we don't know for certain what happened when Philemon finished reading the letter, apparently something wonderful occurred. Onesimus, it seems, proved Paul right, in that he became useful beyond Philemon's imagining. Tradition has it that Onesimus became a tireless laborer, not simply for Philemon, but for Philemon's own master, the Lord of Lords; a leader in the church at Colossae, and, some say, the successor to Timothy as the leader of the believers in Ephesus; and later martyred for the faith.

Roman law was superseded by the grace of God to the benefit of Paul, Philemon, Onesimus himself, and many others whose names we do not know. Grace, as always, proved to be the better way.

People of Hope

It was an amazing sight. A huge man wearing a sweat-soaked wrestling singlet turned a cartwheel. Then a somersault. He rolled up onto his big feet and grinned.

The reason for this unlikely gymnastics display was amazing, too. Rulon Gardner, a farmer from Wyoming, had just defeated Alexander Karelin, the greatest Greco-Roman wrestler the world has ever seen.

Karelin, 285 pounds of skill and muscle, was considered unbeatable. To increase stamina he went on long runs through knee-deep Siberian snow. Even for a big man he was so freakishly strong he frightened the big, tough men who had to compete against him. He often simply yanked them off the wrestling mat and slammed them down as if they were no more than a rolled-up rug or a sack of rice. He was unbeaten in a decade and a half, and had given up two points—yes, two points—in five years.

But now the great Karelin stood at the edge of

the mat in silence, blinking slowly, apparently as dumbfounded as the arena full of wrestling fans who had calculated the possibility of this defeat at about the same odds as ice on the Amazon.

But if Rulon Gardner was surprised, he didn't show it. He had thought all along he could win, he said. "I trained hard," he told sportscaster Jim Gray.

This, it seemed to me, was a striking example of hope: desire combined with expectation. Rulon Gardner had not trained hour upon hour, day after day, week after week, month upon month, expecting to lose. His desire was Olympic gold, and he knew what he needed to do to bring back the medal.

This was no idle fantasy, no mere daydream. He didn't just show up in Sydney and indulge in wishful thinking. He came in the confidence born of disciplined preparation and astute strategy. He would use his size and farmer's strength—he'd been moving stubborn cows for a long time, he explained—to wear his opponents down. And he did.

Desire combined with expectation and resulting in action: this will do as a description of the classic Christian virtue of hope.

Joshua and Caleb, too, had faith defined by hope. They had seen Canaan, and it was good. It flowed with milk and honey. There were clusters of grapes so heavy that it took two men to carry them. They wanted this land, and Jehovah had promised they would have it.

Others weren't so sure. The grapes were impressive, certainly, but so were the Canaanites, big, powerful fighters with the added advantage of the protection of thick city walls. Maybe the grapes would have to remain a tantalizing but futile wish.

And for most of the people, that's all that remarkable fruit ever was. They turned their backs on Canaan, the Land of Promise, and wandered in the desert until they died.

For the brave and patient friends Joshua and Caleb, the result was far different. Joshua led the Children of Israel into their inheritance. And Caleb? After forty years of waiting, he was ready to see his hope fulfilled. "The Lord hath kept me alive..." he said to Joshua. "Now therefore give me this mountain... for thou heardest in that day how the Anakims were there, and that the cities were great and fenced: if so be the Lord will be with me, then I shall be able to drive them out, as the Lord said" (Joshua 14:10, 12). And he did.

For the Christian, hope is bound up with faith.

Abraham, spoken of as a great example of faith, one who "believed God" and was accounted righteous, left his home in Ur because he wanted something better. "I will make of you a great nation," God told him, and Abraham believed Him.

But Abraham had to do something, too. His hope was not inert. He packed up his goods, said goodbye to his prosperous and uneventful life in Ur, organized his family and servants into a caravan, and "went out."

To some, this must have seemed a terribly risky enterprise. Why would anyone abandon comfortable circumstances and head out into the wilderness, into the unknown?

Because of hope. God had given Abraham the desire for something better, and Abraham was confident that God would honor His promise. So out he went, with his camels and goats and at least one nephew and his family, out into the dust and heat—and out of comfortable obscurity into his great place in history, as, all along, he knew he would.

The apostle Paul, too, was a man of hope. He worked hard, confident that his labor would not be in vain. "I planted," he said to the Corinthian believers. "Apollos watered, but God gave the increase."

We, too, look forward with anticipation and expectation to the fulfillment of the promise that illuminates our lives. At dinner nearly two thousand years ago Jesus promised His disciples, "I go to prepare a place for you. And if I go and prepare a place for you, I will come again, and receive you unto myself; that where I am, there ye may be also."

Not long afterward, Luke tells us, these men saw the first part of that promise fulfilled: "While they beheld, he was taken up; and a cloud received Him out of their sight." And two men in white reminded those astonished onlookers, "This same Jesus, which is taken up from you into heaven, shall so come in like manner as ye have seen him go into heaven."

We people of hope look forward to this great event. We desire it. We expect it. Even so come, Lord Jesus.

The Road

We are leaving Jerusalem for Emmaus. The road to Emmaus is one that we know well. It leads *away* — away from hopes that have proven futile, from dreams that have evaporated in the heat of experience, from love that has been betrayed. We are leaving Jerusalem.

In Jerusalem for a few days the longed for but hardly believed things seemed possible. For a few hours in Jerusalem, it seemed that the world of Rome —where the ambitious, the clever, the ruthless, the greedy, always have their way—that world, it seemed, was passing.

There were songs and shouts for one meek and lowly in heart. A king, it was said, who did not subdue men but freed them, who did not take life, but gave it, who insisted that rulers must be servants. Amid the songs and palm branches of Jerusalem, it had seemed possible that from now on everything would be different.

But now, on the Emmaus route, we know better. Reality has settled upon us like the dust of this road.

Deep down, perhaps we knew all along: it will never be different. The ambitious, the clever, the ruthless, the greedy, the hard—they have won. They always win. They always will. Rome, after all, is the eternal city.

Jerusalem has failed us. What is there for us but to leave behind this place of our most cherished and most foolish dreams, and find somewhere inconspicuous, somewhere small and quiet, away from the rush of the history we should never have forgotten? Emmaus will do.

But presently someone walks with us. We scarcely noticed his approach. He is unlooked for, and nothing in us says we have seen him before. But when he speaks there is something—power, undeniable truth, a reminder of what once seemed certain. Surprisingly, on this road to Emmaus, we begin to forget the dust and heat of the journey, the heaviness of our feet, the greater heaviness of our hearts. We listen.

And somehow it is with us as with the blind man who at first glimmer saw men like trees. The darkness falls back, leaving blurred outlines only vaguely perceived by our amazed and delighted eyes. At his words, our confusion and self-pity begin to burn away like fog under the warm sun.

And then, at once, all becomes clear. He blesses bread and breaks it and gives it to us. And we know.

How often has He done this, He the Living Bread, given us what we need, given us Himself? Can there be the smallest doubt? He is alive, and He is with us. He has been, all along.

And all along, the journey endured in fear and sorrow might have been in confidence and joy. What seemed to us as idle tales are true reports.

The One Who walks beside us says to us: "Fear not; I am the first and the last; I am He that liveth, and was dead; and, behold, I am alive for evermore, Amen."

So much for the swagger and boast of Rome, where the proud and ruthless believe that iron can kill truth, that stone can bury it—bury Him. He is alive, He walks beside us, and the grinning Roman certainties, we see, are the delusions of a fool.

And what of Emmaus? Why, Emmaus is forgotten. Once we have seen Him, alive and walking with us, it's plain that every step leads, after all, toward Jerusalem.

The Invitation

"Do you want to get well?"

At first the question might appear silly, or uninformed, or even cruel. Or at best a casual conversation opener, a rhetorical question whose answer is too obvious to warrant a reply. After all, it was asked of a man bedridden for thirty-eight years. He was, apparently, a beggar living with beggars, one of the "great multitude of impotent folk, of blind, halt, withered," a poor and ragged colony of street people who gathered daily near the sheep market at the pool of Bethesda.

I thought of these hapless souls one afternoon as I walked down San Francisco's Haight Street, made famous in the sixties as a center of youthful counterculture.

It is still a place that attracts lost children, adolescents who show up in baggy cast-off clothing, toting a sleeping bag and perhaps leading a dog. They bed down on the sidewalk, backs curled against the sharp San Francisco wind, sleeping as best they can among the other derelicts of the area, the stunned, the alcoholic, the plainly mad.

Frequently Kevin, my friend and son-in-law, who lived several blocks up the hill from Haight, wrapped up part of his dinner and left it on a mailbox or fire hydrant on Haight Street, knowing that it would be wolfed down by the first hungry street camper who happened by.

But our story takes place near the sheep market of Jerusalem. It's a melancholy sight, this neighborhood of the damaged, the unemployable, the hopeless. For these people there is no likelihood that tomorrow will be better than today. They have no plans. Planning assumes resources, and they have only what passerby, people with sharp eyes and strong legs, might drop into the beggar's cup, maybe enough for a simple dinner, maybe not.

And then, suddenly, unexpectedly, the question: "Do you want to get well?" A question, as it turns out, neither casual nor uninformed nor idly curious. It is serious and straightforward, and demands a serious answer. And the answer is not obvious.

There are reasons why the reply might be no. To be sure, the cripple's life is miserable, but it's what he is used to. For almost four decades he has been defined by his disease. Who will he be if not the crippled man?

And if he chooses to be whole he will lose his neighborhood, his "support group," in modern jargon. He has been here by the pool for years. This has been his place, and the blind, the halt and the withered are his friends.

Getting well means, too, that he will lose the right to beg. Then what will he do? He doesn't work. For him there are no immediate job prospects. If he stays on his mat he will probably eat, however simply. If he leaves this place he may not have breakfast.

Albert Camus' powerful novel *The Plague* tells the story of an outbreak of bubonic plague in the Mediterranean port of Oran. Casualties run high, and attempts to combat the epidemic prove exhaustingly ineffective. Many weeks and hundreds of deaths later the outbreak seems to have largely run its course, and two of the story's central characters, the doctor and the journalist, talk quietly together, looking out over the blue sea. "I have realized," Tarrou the journalist remarks, "that we all have plague...no one on earth is free from it." He is speaking now not of bubonic plague, but of the universal human condition, and his diagnosis is correct.

In the Bible the metaphor of sin as disease is persistent and frequent. In the Old Testament, for example, leprosy is often a symbol of sin. And in the New Testament Jesus' healing of a sick or damaged body is frequently emblematic of his healing of a diseased soul. Matthew records that Jesus once said to a paralytic, "Son, your sins are forgiven... Rise, take up your bed and go home" (9:2, 6).

This does not mean that people with defective vision or withered limbs are greater sinners than keen-eyed athletes. It's simply a way of helping us understand our own condition, fallen members of a fallen race, diminished in beauty and power. The poet Keats, already infected with the tuberculosis microbe that would kill him at the age of 27, stood before the powerful and ancient marble statuary excavated in Greece by Lord Elgin and confessed in mortal frustration that he felt like "a sick eagle looking at the sky."

An apt description of a race created in the image of God, now not only capable of every deviance but loving it, addicted to it even as it cripples us.

So the question remains: Do you want to get well? It's the question Jesus asks every one of us. And all too frequently the answer is no. For some, illness has become customary, too familiar to relinquish, too much a part of their identity to renounce. For them the price of health is too high.

Not so the man at the pool. "Rise, take up thy bed, and walk," Jesus says, a startling order to a man who had not been on his feet in thirty-eight years. It must have seemed to an onlooker that this was an invitation to embarrassment and injury, a red face or even a cracked head. Outrageous. Impossible.

But Jesus never tells us to do what He will not enable us to do. And the man on the mat rises, rises to a new life. For years he has gazed at people's feet; now he looks them in the eye. For years his world has been a few square yards of pavement; now he can explore the whole city, the whole country. For years he has survived on the kindness of strangers; now he can earn his own living. At the word of the Great Physician he is whole. He leaves the place of his illness and hopelessness, a new life of strength and promise beckoning him.

I like to think he danced away with the words of the poet king singing in his ears:

> *Bless the Lord, O my soul*
> *And all that is within me,*
> *bless his holy name...*

Who forgiveth all thine iniquities;
Who healeth all thy diseases.

It's the song of a whole man, one who has found his balance, who said yes to the health offered by the Creator. I can't imagine him ever wanting to go back.

Two Sparrows

For Tom Price, who showed me this

The report was—literally—unbelievable. The persistent knocker at the gate in the small hours could not be Peter.

Peter was in a stone cell that was itself inside another stone wall, all doors clamped tight by heavy Roman locks. He was guarded by Roman soldiers, tough, disciplined, armed men who knew their job. Nobody went in or out of that prison without their say so. Certainly not a prisoner on death watch.

The sleepy girl who had answered the knock must have cobwebs in her head. "Go look again."

Shock. Astonishment. It was Peter. At first he had been as surprised and befuddled as anyone else by what had happened—was it a dream, he wondered—while his friends had been praying, perhaps not for his release, but for courage and comfort for the condemned man. He had, after all, denied his Lord on one earlier dangerous occasion.

Their prayers had been answered. Peter had

been having a good night's sleep, and not because he expected to be rescued.

The story in Acts indicates that when the angel came and was finally able to rouse him from his deep and peaceful sleep by thumping him in the ribs, Peter had no idea what was going on. He thought he knew what was going to happen before the sun set again: a rough Roman executioner was going to whack Peter's head off with a heavy blade. It was as good as done.

And Peter had gone to sleep. He was not afraid. He wasn't even worried. There would be no denial, no oaths. He wasn't counting down the passing hours. This was Peter the Rock. He had talked one day with the Risen Lord over breakfast, and everything had changed. Nothing scared him anymore.

He had gone to bed and was fast asleep. It looked to be an easy shift for the guards, two of them linked to Peter by chains, apparently sleeping themselves, and more at the entrance.

And then strange things began to occur, things that no soldier could put in a report, even if he had actually seen it all. An angel sent from God entered the fortress unseen by professional watchmen, came to the prisoner's cell, did something to the locks, roused the man out of his sleep, escorted him back through the prison precincts to the iron gate which swung open by itself, led him out and down the street, and disappeared.

And here Peter was now, at the home of friends, scarcely able to tell what had happened. The solemn prayer meeting, we may imagine, took quite a different turn: hugs, tears, laughter, enough commotion so that Peter had to quiet them all down. Then perhaps there was a raid on the pantry, and the first good meal Peter had enjoyed for a while, maybe cold roast lamb, olives, bread and cheese, dark wine cut with cool water from a stone jar, the simple joys of earth, while he described his miraculous deliverance.

Finally, "Go show these things unto James [the brother of Jesus] and to the brethren," he said, and slipped out into the dark.

It's a wonderful story, full of suspense and adventure. It speaks of God's power over the designs of even the most powerful mortals. It reminds us that no matter how hopeless our circumstances seem He has promised never to forsake us. No wonder we like to tell it.

But let's not forget how the story of Peter's great escape began: "Now about that time Herod the king stretched forth his hands to vex certain of the church.

And he killed James the brother of John with the sword. And because he saw it pleased the Jews, he proceeded further to take Peter also" (Acts 12:1-3).

Let's remember that James, too, had sat in a Roman cell under a death sentence. There had been guards outside his door, too. And when the morning came he was still in chains, and he was taken to the executioner's block and his head was hacked from his body. No delivering angels, no door mysteriously opening, no joyful reunion with his friends who surely were praying for him.

How are we to understand this? We might say that God had prepared Peter to do a great work, to be a pillar of the early church, to preach and to write, and that He would not allow Herod, and the Roman military-police force, to frustrate His intentions. And we would be right.

But James had undergone all the preparation that Peter had. He was one of the twelve, too. More than that, he was one of the special three, the James of Peter, James and John. He, like Peter, had seen Jesus transfigured. Like Peter he had gone apart with Jesus in Gethsemane the night of Jesus' arrest. James was one of the Sons of Thunder who, like Peter, had been with Jesus from the earliest days of his earthly ministry. Surely God had plans for James, too.

Well, yes, but not the same plans He had for Peter. For James there would be no discussions with the former Saul of Tarsus, now Paul the apostle, no speeches at the Council of Jerusalem, no epistles from James lending counsel and support to the early people of the Way. There was to be a beheading.

Perhaps James had overheard the exchange between Peter and Jesus when Peter was told that one day—not the day chosen by Herod, as it turned out, but one day—he would be taken "whither thou wouldest not." Peter asked about John, "Lord, and what shall this man do?" and perhaps James remembered Jesus' answer: "What is that to thee? Follow thou me."

As surely as Peter followed Jesus when he led and fed the Lord's sheep, James followed Jesus to the executioner's block. It may be that in those final hundred steps, then fifty, then twenty, then none, he was thinking of Jesus' words about two sparrows: "Are not two sparrows sold for a farthing? and one of them shall not fall on the ground without your Father."

Released from the cage, one bird flew. One bird fell. Both were in the care of God.

None of us knows where our walk with Jesus

will take us, except to heaven. We are simply called to obedience. And all we know for certain is this: whether in life or in death we are the Lord's.

Great Expectations

A glance through any consumer-oriented magazine is enough to demonstrate how highly our society values convenience—the quick and the easy: quick and easy desserts, quick and easy meals, quick and easy weight loss. "Take a pill and lose ten pounds a week without exercise and without hunger." (This is on the same page as the quick and easy meals.)

A book called *The One-Minute Manager* claims that if you follow a certain formula for a minute a day you too can be a successful executive. Just think of all the time, money and effort you can save by *not* going to Harvard Business School. There's a similar book on how to be a good parent; just follow a few simple instructions.

These instructions may work on imaginary children. Unfortunately, *real* kids wreck their bikes, break their arms, color on the walls, throw up in their beds, tell lies, assault their siblings, insult their teachers, argue, complain and, when they get old enough, take your razor, your comb and your shoes because they can't find their own. And if you are brave enough to poke your head into their room, you'll *know* why they can't find theirs. It's all *probably* there somewhere—or, then, it may not be. It may be at a friend's house or someplace between the front door and the refrigerator.

It would be wonderful if parents could deal with all of this in sixty seconds a day, but such a possibility seems about as likely as discovering a course of cheap, perfectly safe, pollution-free energy or finding a Stradivarius in the attic.

We would all like life to be more tidy, more convenient. That's why the people who write books on how to make it that way get rich. They wish us to believe that there's an easy answer for vexing and continuing perplexities, a secret that they have discovered and will pass along to us for a mere $24.95 hardback.

In our more lucid moments we chuckle over such outrageous flim-flammery. But I wonder if we don't often expect—even suggest—that the Christian life ought to yield itself up to a simple formula.

We'd like it to be easy and convenient. If we just get the knack of it, just figure out the secret, our harassed, sweaty, clumsy and uncertain lives will instantaneously and permanently be carefree, cool, graceful and sure.

Well, if it's so easy, if there's a handy formula, how come my Bible has 1,145 pages in it? How come dozens of pages tell about righteous people who had a hard time? Didn't those folks know the formula? Didn't they listen to the right radio preacher and read the right Christian books? Did not their church have the right program?

Well, there is no secret or foolproof program. Certainly there are good and helpful radio preachers, some good Christian books, some useful plans for church growth. But there is no simple formula. There is only a process. And it's not a neat, shiny mechanical one that can be switched on at the touch of a convenient button. The Bible presents Christian growth as a sustained effort—one that takes time, energy and persistence.

Biblical metaphors for both personal and church growth picture processes that are not quick and easy, like flipping a light switch. Rather, they show work that is long, demanding and strenuous.

Paul, for instance, speaks of his work in establishing the church in Corinth as being like a farmer plowing and planting (1 Corinthians 3:6).

Apollos followed, irrigating and tending the field Paul had sown. They, like the farmer, worked hard and persistently. But ultimately, Paul says, they, like the farmer, waited upon God to do what no human can do: cause the seed to germinate, the stalk to grow, the fruit to appear.

Certainly informed agricultural technique is important. And intelligent planning for church growth is as important as putting fungus-resistant seed in wet areas and heat-hardy crops in dry, hot acreage. But no farmer supposes that the hard work is over if only he plants wisely. What lies ahead is persistent, steady work and the measured seasons of growth and harvest.

Peter speaks of the Christian life as analogous to human growth; the development from infancy to strong maturity. Again, while human growth should be understood, planned for and stimulated, there is no way to speed the process. Nor should there be. Years of nourishment and nurture are required for helpless babies to grow into strong men and women.

As any parent knows, these years are marked by times of pain and struggle. It's not easy being a parent, and it's not easy being a child. For the parents there are sleepless midnights exorcising nightmare monsters, groggy mornings on the way to barn or office to earn the means for the child's food and clothing, evenings spent straining to remember old geometry lessons. There is the effort of sustained discipline: by the exercise of power on occasion, by the force of example always.

For children there are painful jaws as teeth come in, the bruises and occasional broken bones that come with the rough and tumble at the playground or ball field. There are long hours of school, music lessons and religious instruction. There are mothers ladling out broccoli, fathers handing out rakes, orthodontists tightening braces, coaches bellowing out the count for push-ups.

There's nothing easy about any of this. Nobody reaches maturity without enormous effort sustained over a long time. It takes better than a quarter of our life span to reach physical adulthood and a good deal longer to gain emotional and social maturity. (It's surprising, by the way, how hard it is for some people to understand why nineteen-year-old Christian college students don't always act like forty-year-old deacons. Give the kids some time; in another twenty-one years they should act forty. What's really disturbing is forty-year-old deacons behaving like nineteen-year-old college kids.)

Other Bible metaphors for the Christian life carry the same idea of long, persistent effort. There is the figure of building (1 Corinthians 3:9), of a journey (Isaiah 30:21), of a distance race (Hebrews 12:1-2), and of hard combat (Ephesians 6:10-18). Scripture commands us to "study," "run" and "contend."

No, there is no sixty-second method for a strong Christian life, no gimmick or formula for instant maturity. There is no secret about what God wants from us. The crown of righteousness is for those who have persevered, fought the fight, run the course and kept the faith.

Don't bother looking for shortcuts. There are none.

Don't Be Anxious

In *A Fine and Pleasant Misery,* "cautionary tales" of the outdoors, humorist Patrick McManus has an essay on getting lost in the woods. He observes that all experts agree on the first rule for a lost hiker or hunter. It is also, McManus points out, a perfectly useless piece of advice: When you realize you're lost, don't panic. "Oh, sure," McManus says. "As if you had any control over it. Don't panic. You may as well say, 'Don't sweat.'"

The apostle Paul wrote to the believers at Philippi what might at first seem a similarly cavalier piece of advice: Do not be anxious about anything. Right, we might reply. Don't sweat. Great advice.

Well, it's not just advice. It's an admonition. It's an instruction that is supposed to be followed. But how? Can we help it if we panic, sweat and are anxious? Maybe we can. If this is an order there must be some way to carry it out. The Bible indicates that there is.

But first, let's consider what we worry about. I'm

guessing that the list includes plenty of necessary things: money, maybe. You have bills to pay, and so do I. We have to eat, and so do our kids. Some of our kids eat a lot. And their feet grow. They crash bikes and break arms—maybe at the same time. All this costs money, and it's easy to worry about where it's going to come from. And sometimes—let's be honest, now—we fret about not having the money for stuff we really *don't* need, another pair of shoes, a newer car, a bigger house.

I'm not suggesting vows of poverty. I am suggesting that in the age of the consumer, an age when kids murder other kids for their basketball shoes, we remind ourselves that our things are not us, and that we read again the assurance of Jesus in the Sermon on the Mount: "Your heavenly Father knoweth that ye have need of all these things." Anxiety over our bank balance, our popularity, or our success will stunt our growth as human beings, and as children of God.

But I wonder if the very thing that should lower our anxiety level—our relationship with God—doesn't for many people create not less anxiety, but more. I know this is true for some of my students. Their Christian life is not a happy one; rather, it occasions fear, discouragement, frustration and sense of failure.

It seems to me that this is because of wrong ideas about God, God's will, and the nature of the Christian life.

They are inclined to see God as stern, capricious, and overbearing, the great killjoy in the sky. The Israelites fretted and murmured because they became convinced that God was toying with them. "Brought us out here to die," they accused, when He was leading them to freedom. Some think it's very difficult to figure out what God wants us to do, but if we don't get it, if we're not "in His will," we will be in a lot of trouble.

Let's remind ourselves that He calls Himself shepherd, husband, and Father, that He looked on His creation and called it good, and cared enough about it to redeem it after it veered into rebellion and ruin. Let's remember that the story of Jonah is not about a heavy-handed deity smacking around a Jewish prophet until he knuckled under; it's about the persistent love and mercy of a God who intends that a degraded, vicious and bloody people should come to Him and be clean and whole.

Anxiety about being "in His will" stems, I think, from some mistaken ideas about what that means.

One of my former students told me how she

used to fret over what I call the "one and only one myth": there was one person, one place, one job God had picked out for her. She didn't know who or what they were, but thought she had better figure it out or her whole life would be wrong.

The stakes were pretty high. It wasn't just *her* Christian life she was worried about. After all, if she married the wrong man they'd have the wrong kids, the wrong grandkids and—well, you see the problem. Generation after generation until the rapture would be out of God's will—and they'd all be in the wrong place, doing the wrong thing. All because of Liz.

Now it's true that God indicated to Abraham's servant that Rebecca was to be Isaac's wife. He once told Paul to go west, not east. But to most of us He simply says, "Do not be unequally yoked," and "Follow me." "If you love me," Jesus says, "keep my commandments." And, we're told, "His commandments are not grievous."

Nor need the Christian life be thought of as a demand for perfection that is certain to paralyze us. A colleague of mine points out that the Christian life is a direction, a process. Paul admits his own shortcomings, but points out that our sins and failures are not the places where we should stop.

"Forgetting those things which are behind, and reaching forth unto those things which are before, I press toward the mark of the high calling of God in Christ Jesus." A robust Christian life begins with an acceptance of our forgiveness.

And in the same letter Paul tells us how to stop living a life of anxiety. "Be anxious for nothing; but in every thing by prayer and supplication with thanksgiving let your requests be made known unto God."

Prayer provides perspective. Can we seriously pray for Wall Street to enjoy an unending bull market so we can retire early and work on our golf game?

Laboratory studies have demonstrated, too, that prayer is good for our health. Prayer, researchers have learned, lowers blood pressure and produces alpha brain waves, indicative of tranquility, creativity and a sense of well-being.

Let's note that Paul prescribes prayer of a particular kind: it is strongly flavored with thanksgiving.

The results of thankful prayer? "The peace of God, which passes all understanding, shall keep your hearts and minds through Jesus Christ" (Philippians 4:7). We will feel better and think more clearly.

Feeling anxious? There really is something to be done about it. Grateful prayer isn't just casual advice. It's a prescription. And it works.

Undoing the Damage

February 2008

The president of France caused a fuss when he declared that French workers need to work harder and longer. The French thirty-five hour work week, he said, has weakened the French economy. He proposed a fifteen percent increase in hours, which would bring the French work week in line with the American one, increase productivity, and allow French workers to better save for retirement.

Widespread opposition to this policy by French workers and their unions strikes many Americans as one more example, along with the five-week French vacation, of how a former world power has lapsed into self-indulgence. This criticism may have some merit, but the response of one Frenchman I heard on the radio had some merit too. "I don't need more money," he said. "I want time with my family."

A few days before the French work week story, I had caught part of an interview with a researcher—an American—whose study seemed to show that we

Americans work too much and rest too little, and that in the long run our long hours actually reduce our productivity. We need to get away from work, he said, for a minimum of two weeks at a time to renew our brains.

This perspective seemed in keeping with what my friend Dr. Bill McVaugh, whose neurobiological research has included studies on sleep, once told me about the function of sleep. The purpose of sleep is not so much to rest the body as it is to restore and recharge the brain, he said. People who ignore or scant their built-in sleep requirements are headed toward serious trouble, including loss of productivity, illness, and depression. "If you lose sleep," Bill told me, "you have to make it up hour for hour."

Why do Americans work longer hours than many other people? And is that sort of schedule a virtue or a bad habit? And what does the Bible have to say about this value placed on long hours of work?

I suspect there are a number of answers to the first question: why? One answer is historical. When European colonists arrived in North America, there was a lot to be done. English gentlemen at Jamestown who thought manual labor was beneath them might have all died if Captain John Smith had not cracked the whip and made them work. Later colonists worked hard to clear land, build simple homes, plant crops, hunt and fish, and organize communities.

Two hundred years later the "emigrants" from the American East who struggled over the Oregon Trail into the Willamette Valley, where I live, repeated the pattern. There really was no choice; you worked very hard or you and your family perished.

Americans have been a resourceful and productive people. Necessity long ago became a virtue and the benefits of that virtue have been impressive—we eat well, we have large, comfortable homes and comfortable cars, and our hospitals are equipped with a remarkable array of medical technology.

All this is expensive, and we expect to work hard to live this way. But when is enough enough? When is the house big enough? When is the car new enough? When do we have enough money?

Put another way, when can we stop working and enjoy the fruits of our labor? When is it time to rest?

The Bible offers precepts and models that speak to these questions. Many of the Biblical proverbs warn against sloth. Paul ordered the Christians at Thessalonica, "Work with your own hands...that ye may walk honestly toward them that are without, and that ye may have lack of nothing" (1 Thessalonians 4:11-12). Paul himself modeled the life of industry, making tents to support himself while establishing the church at Corinth.

But as in all things, balance is the rule. God established the Sabbath for a reason: there is a time to work and a time to stop working. A glance at the instructions given to Israel for their new life in the Promised Land included a lot of time away from work —not only the seventh day of every week, but frequent holidays and festivals.

Instructions for observing the Passover include this: "In the first day shall be an holy convocation [a sacred assembly]; ye shall do no manner of servile [regular] work therein." The same for the Feast of Weeks, the Feast of Trumpets, the Day of Atonement, and the Feast of Tabernacles (Numbers 28, 29). Every fiftieth year too was set apart as a year of restoration; debts were cancelled, everyone returned to the family property, and no one was to plant crops.

I'm not suggesting these Old Testament Israelite practices be adopted by modern Americans, or even what kinds of adaptations might be necessary for a post-industrial service economy rather than an agrarian one. I'm simply pointing out that there are

Biblical expectations for rest as well as for work. Jesus Himself, let's remember, often withdrew from His busy days of teaching and healing to rest, think, and pray.

I know a thoughtful pastor who has taken a look at the busy schedule of his church and of many others and has begun to wonder if all the activities—every one established with the best of intentions—might have reached the point of saturation, might even have come to damage the life of the church. Maybe, he told me, we have become so scheduled, so busy, that we hardly have time to genuinely and naturally enjoy the Lord and enjoy each other. Maybe there's a danger of getting caught up, like Martha, with physical activities at the expense of the spirit.

Not long ago I was given formal recognition for many busy years of professional service. It was a generous gesture, a genuine honor, and I appreciated it. Then something especially delightful happened. My wife got a phone call from a lifelong friend of mine who had been at the occasion. She and her sisters were planning an evening to express their own affection and happiness for what had been given to me.

We ate barbecued burgers and salads, and remembered old times. Five of the eight people there were musicians, and after dinner they gathered around the piano and sang and played Cole Porter tunes and gospel songs.

"Savior, like a shepherd lead us," sang my wife in her clear, sweet soprano, while Judy and Paul improvised accompaniment on piano and muted trumpet, "much we need Thy tender care. In Thy pleasant pastures feed us; for our use Thy folds prepare. Blessed Jesus...Thine we are."

Then the three sisters gave me a box wrapped in silver and black. Inside the box rested a pair of small books that had belonged to their father, a college buddy of my own dad, a man who for many years before his death had been like an uncle to me. Inside the cover of one of them were a few words in his handwriting.

Darkness gathered and it was time to go. It had been a wonderful evening, unscripted, natural, easy-paced and joyful, a restful time apart from what Walt Whitman called "the tugging and hauling" of a busy life. I felt at peace, renewed, refreshed.

I need more evenings like this. We all do.

Power Restored

I arrived home on the first hot day of the year to find that the house was without power. My household was, the newspaper reported the next day, one of about ten thousand customers left without electricity because of a failed insulator. The paper noted that the outage knocked out traffic signals at several major intersections, creating "chaos at rush hour."

Things were fouled up at home, too. Dirty laundry lay in a heap in front of the useless washing machine. The house was getting hot, and of course the fans wouldn't work. The TV room in the basement was cool, but the television was out of commission, and without lights it was too dim down there to read. I began to worry about the food in the freezer, and my grandson and I decided we should eat the ice cream before it melted. He took the French vanilla and I finished off the butter pecan.

The computer was laid up, too. But the biggest problem was water. We live at the edge of town in a house built when this was countryside, and we get our water from a well. The electric pump was out, of course, and we began to see how important that was. The toilet tank could not refill. The morning's dirty dishes stayed dirty. And on an afternoon with temperatures in the mid-nineties, so did we. There were no showers for our hot, sticky bodies.

What to do for dinner? We considered hot dogs roasted on our little backyard barbecue but decided to drive to a nearby restaurant where we could eat and use the bathroom.

The main electrical failure had produced a ripple effect, the smaller stations directing power to individual neighborhoods going down like dominos. But the men in hard hats worked on into the warm night, and finally power and order were restored. This morning the washing machine is humming as the pile of dirty laundry shrinks. There's ice in the freezer and cool milk in the fridge. At the touch of a button I fill the house with music.

I've had a hot breakfast of soft-boiled eggs on toast with three slices of bacon cooked crisp in the microwave. And best of all, I'm clean—yesterday's sweat and fret sluiced down the drain by a rush of hot, healing water. It is, as Mr. Rogers liked to say, a beautiful day in the neighborhood.

I've been reminded about what happens when the electron flow that does so much to make our lives clean, comfortable, and productive is interrupted; about the chaos, misery, and difficulty of lives without power; about what happens, for instance, when not just electrical lines but human beings short out; about what happened in Eden when there occurred a catastrophic spiritual power outage and the line between the Creator and the creatures came down; about the sweat and dirt and disease that followed; about the chaos of a world "off-line," and all the painful effects of the original and massive power outage.

I've been reminded, too, that if I meant to restore my home to order there was only one way to do it: I had to have the power back. There was just no other way, no other plan, no other process. I had to get reconnected.

I've been thinking about the One Who said, "All power is given unto me" and the ways He intends to direct that power through every believer to bring light to a darkened world, warmth to cold hearts, living water to thirsty souls. For the gospel, Scripture reminds us, is "the power of God unto salvation to every one that believeth."

Reviewing

On the screen the Sunday School superintendent swung a sledgehammer in time to "The Anvil Chorus," then to a pop song of the sixties, "That's the sound of the men/Working on the chain gang." And there we were pictured, with wheelbarrows, picks and shovels, the foundation for the fellowship hall where we now sat, dinner over, reviewing what the year of prayer, giving and hard work had accomplished.

On the screen, rain poured down. Watching it, we nudged each other: "Remember that day? By noon I thought I'd never be warm or dry again." And now, to the strains of the "Hallelujah Chorus," we again watched the high framed walls being slowly lifted into place. "I was praying hard," our assistant pastor said. "I was scared the wall might go right on over. The Lord was good."

This video was our Ebenezer, our reminder of the ways that the Lord had "hitherto helped us." The tape had been shot week by week by two members of our church and then edited and produced by another, a man who works for a television station and has his own production company. The tape is in our church library, available to the congregation, a memorial to good work and an encouragement for the next project.

The technology is new, but the principle goes back thousands of years. The children of Israel, because they were like us, were prone to forget what God had done for them. They forgot about their deliverance from slavery and from the world's best soldiers, who chased them to take them back to Egypt. They forgot about the water from the rock. And because they forgot, they feared.

At the crucial moment, the greatest moment of their lives, the moment when, born slaves, they could have taken the land God had promised them and live as free men, they balked.

Over the next forty years, one by one they died—all but two—not as slaves but as those akin to vagabonds. They had nothing to leave their children but an account of fear and failure.

At last, near Jericho, the Israelites had their chance again. The Jordan River was at flood stage, but at the Lord's command they stepped into the stream—and the flow stopped. They crossed on dry land.

Then there was one more thing to do. "Take you

twelve men out of the people," the Lord told Joshua, "...and command ye them, saying, Take you hence out of the midst of Jordan...twelve stones...and leave them in the lodging place, where ye shall lodge this night" (Joshua 4:2-3).

The reason? "When your children ask their fathers in time to come, saying, What mean ye by these stones? Then ye shall answer them, that the waters of Jordan were cut off before the ark of the covenant of the Lord...and these stones shall be for a memorial unto the children of Israel forever" (Joshua 4:6-7).

Imagine the joy of telling the story. "Abba, why are these stones here?"

"Son, those stones were put there on the most amazing day of my life. That one closest to you—yes, that one—your Uncle Eli brought up from the middle of the river, right out there where you see that swirl. Except on that day it was dry. Let me tell you what the Lord did for us that day..." It was a story the boy needed to hear and the father needed to tell, so that this time there would be no forgetting.

Monuments to success are heartening. We need them. But there's another kind of marker, another sort of memorial, calling up stories that—while bringing no joy in the telling—are as important as our tale of stones by the Jordan.

Some of these memorials have names like Auschwitz, Buchenwald and Dachau. We must tell our children what these names signify and what happened in the gas rooms and the ovens. We must explain the meanings of the words above the gates: "Nicht Niemals." Never again. We *must* tell them if "Nicht Niemals" is to be more than a fervent wish.

There are those who claim that the Holocaust never happened, that the accounts of bestiality and slaughter are nothing more than propaganda. But the ovens are there to say that these men lie. They are there to remind us of the consequences of sin, of what human beings are capable of apart from God, and of what danger may befall our children if we forget or allow them to.

These hideous memorials must be understood not only as monuments to the meaning of sin, important as that is. They must as well be markers of commitment. "Never again."

God Himself spoke these words as a commandment to mankind and all life on Earth. "Neither shall all flesh be cut off any more by the waters of a flood," He said to Noah. "...I do set my bow in the cloud, and it shall be for a token of a covenant between me and the earth... When I bring a cloud over the earth...the bow shall be seen in the cloud: and I will remember my covenant, which is between me and you and every living creature of all flesh" (Gen. 9:13-15).

In Oregon, spring is the season of rainbows and cherry blossoms and wedding invitations. Because I am a college teacher, and because I like my students, my mail includes invitations to weddings.

My wife and I attend as many as we can, partly because we have been honored by the invitation, and partly for another reason: it's good for us to remember. As the young bride and groom join hands and repeat their vows, I remember the words I said more than four decades ago to the woman beside me: "For better, for worse; for richer, for poorer; in sickness and in health; 'til death do us part."

I touch her left hand and she smiles. She knows. I'm saying it all again. It's important to remember.

Conversations with My Students

The Principle of Nearest at Hand
April 2003

I had just forked up my first bite of lasagna when Charlene moved out of the busy dining hall traffic and stopped at my table.

"Do you have a few minutes to talk to a senior?"

"Sure," I said. "Set your tray down here. We'll talk while we eat." I had a pretty good idea what the topic would be. It was late April, only three weeks from commencement. I'd had these conversations before.

"Graduation scaring you a little?" I asked.

"Yes."

"Not sure what you're going to do next?"

A hesitant smile. "No, I'm not." She seemed apologetic, as if she were owning up to a social error or a character flaw. "I just don't know what to do."

"Tell me your options," I said. She named several, and they all sounded good. She wasn't considering a career as an embezzler or a bank robber, and she wasn't planning to marry one.

"These all sound good," I said. "What's the

problem?" I knew, of course, what the problem was.

For four years she had worked hard, pressing on toward a clearly defined goal. She was going to earn that degree. Life wasn't always easy. There were books to read, exams to take, and papers to write. Lots of them. There were some long days and short nights. But she knew where all this was going and what she had to do to get there.

And she had done it. Now what?

I invited her to consider the Principle of Nearest at Hand. This was the principle given to Saul of Tarsus on the road to Damascus. "What do you want me to do?" he asked Jesus, Whom he had been persecuting. A good question, and under the circumstances, the only one to ask.

The long answer would one day be impressive. It would include establishing churches all around the Mediterranean coast; undertaking the first Christian mission to pagan Europe; assuming an authoritative position in the early church; defining and defending the status of Gentile believers; preaching before scholars, governors, and the emperor; and writing nearly half of the New Testament.

All this, of course, was years down the road. And Saul was told nothing about any of it. He was told something very simple: "Go to Damascus." That's all.

Damascus was right down the road. Ephesus and Philippi and Athens were a long way off, and though Saul (soon to be Paul) didn't know it, the route to them ran through Damascus. Without going to Damascus, he couldn't get to Corinth and Rome. Damascus was nearest at hand.

The same Principle of Nearest at Hand applies, as well, to judging. Nathan the prophet came to King David with a story of a crime. There was a poor man, Nathan said, who owned a single lamb. It was a pet, his constant companion. His neighbor, rich and powerful, owned large flocks. But when a friend paid a visit to his estate, the wealthy man, rather than take one sheep out of the flock for a special dinner, sent some muscular hired hands to rob his poor neighbor of his single pet lamb. What, Nathan asked, should be done about this?

David, king and chief justice, was outraged at the crime and the callousness and greed of the perpetrator. It's easy to picture his fiery eyes as he leaned forward in his judge's chair and bellowed, "Such a man should die!"

David had a warm heart and a passionate sense of justice. That such a thing should happen in his kingdom! In his own city!

The crime scene, it turned out, was even closer than that. The outrage had occurred right here, and the criminal was none other than the judge himself. "Thou art the man," Nathan said, and suddenly everything became clear to the judge. He was indeed guilty, and not just of stealing a pet lamb. David, who had a whole harem of beautiful and important women, had stolen a friend's wife and then had arranged the man's death.

His sense of justice and moral outrage had not disappeared; he had simply failed to judge nearest at hand. "You hypocrite," Jesus said to those who were quick to indict others for their shortcomings. "First cast the beam out of your own eye. Then maybe you can see to get the speck out of your brother's."

In other words, make it a habit to judge nearest at hand.

The same principle applies to claims of Christian love. If we say we love God but despise our brother or sister in Christ, the Bible says we are kidding ourselves. John put it this way: "If a man say, I love God, and hateth his brother, he is a liar: for he that loveth not his brother whom he hath seen, how can he love God whom he hath not seen?" (1 John 4:20;

compare Mark 12:29-31).

It won't do, for instance, to belt out hymns or praise songs on Sunday morning and whisper malicious gossip on Monday.

Loving nearest at hand has other practical consequences too. Consider these words, again from John: "But whoso hath this world's goods, and seeth his brother have need, and shutteth up his bowels of compassion from him, how dwelleth the love of God in him?" (1 John 3:17).

James is similarly blunt: "If a brother or sister be naked, and destitute of daily food, and one of you say unto them, Depart in peace, be ye warmed and filled; notwithstanding ye give them not those things which are needful to the body; what doth it profit?" (James 2:15-16).

Jesus outlined the same principle in the Great Commission: first Jerusalem, then Judea and Samaria. Then the ends of the earth.

There's no need for anyone to be anxious about what God wants us to do or where He wants us to go. There are things for us to do right where we are. When we are about our Father's business and caring for His children right here, right now, we are doing what He wants us to do, right where He wants it done.

Consider This...

October 1993

On the charts for a month or so in 1960 was a funny song about a timid member of Custer's Seventh Cavalry. As the troops ride toward the Little Bighorn he trails along at the dusty end of the column, complaining, protesting and, as a kind of refrain, bleating, "What am I doin' here?"

All of us who have gone to college have asked ourselves the same question. As we slog along through a choking cloud of lectures, papers, exams, speeches and projects we croak, "What am I doin' here?" Bills pile up, our shoes wear thin, deadlines loom, laundry begins to mold. The coach announces extra practice, the boss schedules extra work hours, the girl back home hints that she needs more attention. And nobody forced this kind of life on us; we volunteered. "What am I doin' here?" we ask.

The friend who stayed home and took the job at the warehouse has a new pickup with a great sound system. He's playing softball three nights a week, and he can afford to take a girl—never mind which one—out for the best steak in town. Our last night out was a month ago, to the pizza parlor. "What," we ask again, "what am I doin' here?"

Good question. And there are a number of good answers. For one thing, you're increasing your earning power by fifty percent or more. You're broke now, but that degree is worth a lot more than its weight in gold. The numbers suggest that before long the guy who stayed in the warehouse will have to work year-round to make what you'll have earned by the end of August.

Too, you are ensuring the chance to make choices. You will not have to work in the warehouse if you don't want to—or at least not for long. You are gaining the skills that will allow you to pursue a career, not just hold down a job.

But money issues aside, you are here for several compelling reasons. You're learning to be human—to know, to think, to speak, and to walk like redeemed sons and daughters of God, in dignity and strength.

You are preparing for leadership. You have the chance, as many others do not, to acquire the skills and perspective to influence your community for good.

So stay with the work. You are in the right place. You are doing the right thing. Keep on.

A Brave Heart for the Future

April 2004

Here you are, four years of school behind you, sheepskin in hand, headed out the door, full of hopes and fears as you get ready for the big wide scary wonderful world.

And after that long introductory sentence—longer than I've coached you to write—I have one final chance as your professor and friend to offer some unsolicited advice.

So here it is: I'm advocating unsensitivity training. In a society where all manner of weeping, shouting groups claim victimhood for themselves, for some other group, or for beast, fish and fowl, a society in which holier-than-thou has been superseded by more-sensitive-than-thou as the mark of the post-modern Pharisee, I ask you—*urge* you—to develop a cooler eye, a steadier pulse and a thicker skin than what is fashionable.

Here's why.

First, there's big money now in the evangelical

sub-culture of which you and I are a part. I mean big money—as in multi-million dollar recording contracts, sold out sports arenas at $40 a seat when Christian celebrity speakers come to town, $1,000 prayer tickets (called things like "seed offerings"—send the money and an expensively coiffed character posing as a real preacher will, he promises, pray for your prosperity) and, as recently reported in newspapers across the nation, a $42 million contract recently negotiated with a major publisher by a best-selling preacher-speaker-author. Serious cash.

Some of you have some talent in music, in writing, in business. In an age where wealth, stardom and celebrityhood are the siren songs that lure too many onto spiritual and emotional rocks, I hope you will keep your wits about you, remember what Jesus said about all that, and steer a steadier, if less glamorous, course than stardom often requires.

And I urge you to grow a thick skin because you will surely encounter trying circumstances. I don't mean mid-term exam trying; I mean your boss tells you to cook the books if you want to keep your job trying; I mean your husband tells you he no longer finds you attractive and there's someone at work trying; I mean waiting for the biopsy report trying.

Paul tells us to endure hardness as good soldiers. When bullets and shrapnel are buzzing and whining about our heads we can't worry about mosquitoes. Sensitivity has its place, but sometimes you will be called upon to serve your Lord with a cool head and a brave heart, to ignore petty itches and even to carry on though seriously wounded.

James says we should consider it all joy when we encounter difficult trials—not because we're masochists, but because difficulties are the mileposts on the long hard road to wisdom. It's a road I urge you, with all the love, respect and hope I have for you, to walk without flinching.

Jesus walked it before you, sunburned, foot-bruised and sweating. And so strong that a tomb in a rock could not contain Him.

"Be thou strong and very courageous," God said to Joshua, that tough, brave leader of Israel, "for the Lord thy God is with Thee."

He says the same to all of us.

Telling the Truth about Writing

Students at Christian colleges have an especially hard time telling some kinds of truth. We have been taught certain pieties that may not speak truthfully to some of our experiences, and we're reluctant to say so.

Here's an example. Some years ago one of my students cautiously asked if she could write about the unexpected death, six months or so earlier, of her father. As the family prepared for the funeral this girl had understood her pastor to say that there would be non-believers at the ceremony, and it was important for Christians to let them know that Daddy was in heaven, and it was all right.

"Well," she told me, "it's not all right with me!"

Of course it wasn't. Dad was okay, but his daughter certainly was not. She was grieving, as she should have been, and furious that she had not been allowed to grieve properly and publicly.

Perhaps she had not heard her pastor correctly. But it wasn't until she felt free to express her anger and sadness truthfully that she could write the powerful and moving essay that she finally produced. Far from a mere recitation of unconvincing, prefabricated phrases, her essay was an honest account of one human being's shock, pain and fear at the loss of a father who had loved and guided her every day of her life, and whose faithful presence had helped her understand the idea of a heavenly Father.

And now that presence was gone. She was facing an absence that would continue for the rest of her life. Would anyone have believed her if she had shrugged off this blow with a smile and a piety?

I learned long ago that students know pretty quickly whether a teacher likes them. And they can't be fooled. Similarly, readers sense early on whether a writer is trying to tell the truth. They won't be fooled. If what they're reading doesn't ring true, if the writer is trying to look good or appears fearful or lazy, the reader simply stops reading. The conversation between writer and reader is over because the writer has failed the obligation to talk seriously and truthfully.

And a writer has to know things, has to develop and exercise an attentive eye. Thoreau at Walden kept a sharp eye out for things most people miss. As a consequence he left us a fascinating and detailed account of an ant battle, red warriors and black warriors engaged in an insect version of the struggles at Troy. Thor Heyerdahl notes that while passengers on an ocean liner believe they are passing through a lifeless ocean the crew aboard *Kon Tiki,* the raft of balsa logs floating slowly across the Pacific, observed life everywhere and in an astonishing variety of forms, from luminous plankton to great whales.

If we writers expect to offer readers any kind of service we need to know things: which trees grow on the east slopes of the Cascade Mountains, how the presence of elephants alters a biome, what goes into the design and production of a new car model, what actually happens in a team locker room at halftime, how a potato in an Idaho field ends up in an order of fries in California.

We learn by watching, by interviewing, by researching, by listening.

Writers know the coo of a dove, the whistle of a red-winged blackbird and the sharp cry of a red-tailed hawk. And when we're writing about people we listen carefully to volume, tone, and regional dialects. A "brook" in New York is a "crick" in Maine, a "branch" in Kentucky, a "run" in Virginia.

And good writers have an ear for good sentences, for the ways that words in a sentence fall on the ear in patterns and rhythms that lend weight and penetrating power to mere vocabulary. The rhythms of the words of Lincoln and King are part of their great speeches, part of the reason we read them again and again. The cadences of their words at Gettysburg and at Washington carry the weight and power of waves of the sea.

"Yet in a larger sense we cannot dedicate, we cannot consecrate, we cannot hallow this ground."

"I have a dream that one day on the red hills of Georgia, the sons of former slaves and the sons of former slave owners will be able to sit down together at the table of brotherhood."

And how do we develop this ear, this particular way of hearing, of laying words on paper in patterns that add weight and strength to our prose?

By reading. If there's another way I don't know about it. Good writers are readers. They have read the Bible (young Walt Whitman absorbed the rhythms and patterns of Old Testament poetry as his Quaker mother read Scripture aloud), have read Shakespeare and Spenser, Coleridge and Keats, Joyce and Thomas, read Hawthorne and Poe, Fitzgerald and Hemingway, Edward Abbey and Annie Dillard.

This is not to say that good writers copy anyone

else's style. Rather, good writers have taken into themselves the ways that great writers have composed, have developed a sense of how the best English sounds, and have learned to say things their own way, a way that is not imitative of another writer, but is informed by many other writers.

On the basketball court Kobe Bryant is not an imitation of Julius Erving, the great Dr. J. He is physically stronger and has more range. But when Bryant goes to the glass, anybody who saw and appreciated the play of Erving can see the explosiveness and aerial acrobatics that Erving introduced into the game.

Don't worry about developing an original style. If you read a lot, pay attention to what's going on, and try to write clearly and economically you will do it in a way that is yours, just as singers who listen to great singers and study vocal technique will end up sounding like themselves and nobody else.

All this listening and reading and attention to detail is part of the commitment to craft that every good writer has to make. Basketball players spend hours in the gym, good pianists spend hours at the keyboard, and writers—well, writers have to write, and that means revising, rewriting, inspecting every paragraph, every sentence, every word, as carefully and sternly as a drill sergeant inspecting young recruits learning to be United States Marines.

If this sounds like a grind, it isn't. Not for people who care about their craft and art. Great shortstops love to take infield practice, over and over and over; there's joy in it, and in the grace and surety long practice brings.

So there it is, friends. Grab your glove and let's go.

A Word to the Rookies

I once heard Tim Green, the former All-Pro defensive lineman for the Cincinnati Bengals, comment on his rookie year in the NFL. Green, an All-American in college, was a high draft pick and came into the league with natural expectations of success.

What he experienced was a painful shock. This was not the game he was accustomed to. "Everything was speeded up," Green explained. Offensive linemen tore into him so quickly at the snap that he couldn't get himself clear to make a play. Big, powerful running backs ripped past him before he could get in position to make a tackle. Nothing had quite prepared him for the game he was now playing. Green began to wonder if he was going to make it in the NFL.

Then he discovered—as training camp and the exhibition season went on—that the game "slowed down." He was able to fight off blocks, get where he was supposed to be, and make the tackles he was getting paid to make.

Here's why I'm telling you this story. Many students have told me that they have been caught off balance by the work load facing them when syllabi are handed out the first day of class. "That's a lot of reading, isn't it?" some have asked, not so much by way of inquiry as of complaint. "I have other classes, you know."

I know. That's why your professors tell you the very first day what will be happening this term. If you get started right away, plan your study schedule the way college students have to, and work steadily, you will be fine. Those upperclassmen who seem comfortable with their workload? They're not all smarter than you. The game has slowed down for them. They have established work habits that make success normal.

The work load assigned by your professors is normal for this league. The expectation that you will have your reading done when you come to class is normal. The expectation that you will hand in papers on time is normal. So is the expectation that those papers will be thoughtful, clearly organized and grammatically correct.

Some of you will join the game with no trouble at all. Others may find the pace uncomfortably fast at first. Don't let that scare you or discourage you. You may see that you need to adjust your social schedule, or that you have to say no—or not right now—to a number of worthy activities at school or at church, or that you can't go home as often as you would like.

That's normal.

So develop good work habits. Take charge of your time. Get used to reading a lot, listening carefully, and thinking hard. That's the nature of the game here. I'm betting that you're going to like it.

The Loud, Long Cataract of Sound

It's hard to write just now because some kind of heavy equipment, a tamper, I'm guessing, is making a hammering racket at a work site not far from my office, and has been all day. Maybe I should be getting used to it.

For much of the summer earth movers and dump trucks and pavers have been beeping and honking and rumbling a couple of hundred feet from my bedroom window, sometimes during the day, often at midnight.

My head vibrated with my house.

Just part of the cost of living in the machine age, I suppose.

There are tradeoffs for the conveniences of our machinery. Getting from Portland to Los Angeles in just a couple of hours to see my friends is a very noisy event. I like my Camry, and I imagine the factory where it was assembled was every bit as noisy as the plant where I worked the summer of my marriage. Even though I wore the required earmuffs my ears rang long after my shift was over. Maybe that's part of the reason I say "Huh?" and "What?" a dozen times a day.

But research has linked the long, loud cataract of sound that washes over us to more than hearing loss. Some studies point to links with elevated blood pressure, cardiovascular disease and even—yikes!—impotence.

Perhaps when the rain comes the racket of the construction projects will be washed away, at least for a few months.

I hope so.

I have less hope for relief from the elevated sound levels of—well, I'll say it—my church, and I don't mean just the one I attend on Sunday morning, where the first half hour pumps out volume and volubility at levels that are too much for me, but that most of the folks around me seem to like. And I like them, so okay, I deal with it. Maybe I'm just old and out of touch, as usual, with the folkways of Contemporary American Evangelical Christianity.

But I think of my much younger friend Anna, now Sister Teresa, once my best Corban student, now a nun. While doing graduate work at Oregon State she visited St. Mary's Catholic Church. She went again, and then regularly, and in time came to my office to tell me she was converting. "I wanted to tell you myself," she said.

"Thank you," I said. "I appreciate that. And I trust you. You know what you are doing. But I'd like to know why. What did you find at St. Mary's?"

He answer was succinct.

"I found out I prayed better," she said.

I went for a visit, and I saw what she meant. It was quiet enough for me to think, to meditate, to pray. Apparently nobody was uncomfortable with silence; they seemed to welcome it.

Many of my students do not. Some morning this term I'll send my freshmen writers out of doors with these instructions: "No phones, no texting, no talking. Don't take paper or pen. There are no expectations here except one: you must be quiet for eight minutes. *Vaya con Dios.*"

In the past, student elation at being cut loose from class eight minutes early has been tempered for some by the stress of eight minutes of silence, eight minutes with nothing much but their own thoughts. "Just about drove me nuts," they have reported. "Please don't ask me to do that again."

Others, though, have asked how soon we might

repeat the experience. "I never knew there were so many birds around here," one smiling girl said.

Others commented on the calming effects of even eight minutes of quiet—and how rare it was.

There's a lot of noise about the purpose of a college education, a lot of voices in the conversation, including some loud ones sneering at the impracticality of studying philosophy, history, art, literature—fields of study not designed to make the learner a lot of money.

Perhaps you will excuse me for adding one more voice. I promise to keep it down.

Here's what I hope to accomplish at Corban. I hope that because of what you and I do together, the books and poems we read together, the conversations we have in the classroom and on the sidewalk and in the dining hall, maybe the way we stand quietly together looking out over the city to the quiet mountains—that because of this you will learn to be comfortable with yourself and by yourself, that you will be at ease in the world, tuned to its soft but persistent music that is there for anyone with ears to hear it.

Sir Edward Dyer wrote, "My mind to me a kingdom is," and I hope yours will be the same for you. If you choose, you can populate it with Shakespeare's sonnets and Keats's odes and Bach's chorales. And the songs of the birds in the rustling oaks and whispering firs on the campus of Corban University.

Commencement 2013

Dietrich Bonhoeffer explained a lot about the Christian life by observing that a man lying in the arms of his wife should not be thinking about heaven. Funny? Sure. But he wasn't really joking. Far from it. There's great insight here about how humans should please their Creator and Lord, and do His will not only sometime in heaven, but now, on earth.

Pastor Bonhoeffer made the same point when he wrote in one of his letters that he had come to believe that reading *The Song of Solomon* as a love poem—not first as an allegory of God and Israel or of Christ and the Church, but a love poem—was the most Christological reading possible.

What did he mean? Something like this: a life honoring God will be a life of gratitude and gladness for His gifts, gifts given to human beings as the Creator's intentions for the created. And Bonhoeffer said this: these gifts are to be enjoyed when they are meant to be enjoyed, heaven in due season, the sacred joys of earth now.

The Bible is a lot clearer about this than the ascetics that have disparaged the gifts of God since the prissy Pharisees indicted Jesus for being "a glutton and a winebibber." Most of the Old Testament holy days, for example, were feasts, big parties with lots of food. Solomon's instructions to his son enjoined him to revel in the wife of his youth, to be intoxicated with her love. He goes on—more explicitly than I will here. To borrow a phrase from Casey Stengel, "You could look it up."

Here's my point: I hope your graduation is a joyful day that marks the beginning of a joyful life. Your education at Corban should have prepared you for this kind of life.

The big day is almost here. I know that some of you are anxious about what comes next. I am not a prophet—I thought Duke would win the NCAA championship—but I can tell you this: what is about to commence is a great adventure. I can tell you that, like all adventures, it will sometimes require all your courage, all your skills (good thing you've studied hard these four years, isn't it?), every bit of your strength. That's the nature of adventures.

I can tell you this, too: one of God's gifts is a strength beyond your own, the kind of strength that lies at the heart of joy. They that wait upon the Lord, I remind you, will renew their strength, fly with the wings of eagles, run and not be exhausted.

Recently I was in a service when one of the songs claimed that "brokenness" was what the singers "longed for." I didn't believe that for a minute.

The song next asserted that this brokenness was what God wanted from us. I have my doubts about that, too. Jesus said to the crippled man at the pool, "Wilt thou be made whole?" That's what He wants from us. Wholeness. Strength. Joy. That's what redemption is all about.

When you came here you were three months out of high school, just kids, really, uncertain about what to expect. Some of you were pretty scared. How were you supposed to read four hundred dollars' worth of books in one semester? How could you be expected to live in a small room with someone you had never even met? How were you supposed to know what you wanted for a major?

But you made it. You decided. You worked things out. And now you see how your life has been enriched. You can see how strong you've grown.

So after four years together, after four years of training and practice and scrimmages, here's what I want to say to you: The game is about to begin. You're ready to go. Enjoy it.

And that noise you hear in the background? That's me, and the rest of your teachers. We're cheering.

Exit Exam

This is a season of questions—for you: what's next? More school? Look for a job? Travel? Marry?

And for me: professors wonder if we've done you as much good as we had hoped. As you leave Corban, what are you taking with you that we hoped to give?

The big buzz in education over the last couple of decades has been assessment, attempts to measure how much you have learned while you were here.

Sometimes we can get some reliable answers about some things. Education isn't like manufacturing a car. It's hard or impossible to measure educational outcomes the way we can measure the efficiency of combustion or the air drag of a body style. There are too many variables. Still, we can find out if you have learned enough to sit for your CPA exam, or make a reasoned argument.

Other answers are pretty hard to come by: how much did your writing improve because you took Creative Non-Fiction, or did that improvement come about because of something that you read in *The*

Atlantic, or because of a conversation you had with a friend over the summer, or because you picked up Ann LaMott's *Bird by Bird*?

It's impossible to say for sure.

And in any event, the big questions don't show up on any instrument of assessment that I've ever seen—and I don't know as they can. I'm talking about what kind of person you have learned to be these last four years, what you have become as a consequence of thinking, talking, writing and breaking bread with me and with my friends on the faculty here at Corban University, thinking and talking and writing about what it means to be a human being, especially what it means to be a redeemed human being.

It means a good many things, but in an age when Rush Limbaugh and Bill Maher are paid millions for intemperate, ill-mannered and scornful rants; when the Kardashians and the strutting jerks from Jersey Shore become famous for crass, crude, arrogant and childish behavior—the worse the behavior the higher the ratings—and when just about any kind of rude speech is daily fare on social media: when even the F-bomb fails to detonate because we're so used to it, I hope you leave Corban University with humility, love—and grace: grace in your bearing, in your demeanor and treatment of others, and in your speech.

We don't have a test for grace, and we shouldn't. But your friends and neighbors have a fair idea of how you're doing in that department, your wife or husband will have a better one, your children will have an even more sensitive and informed one, and God will know exactly.

A century ago the great Irish poet William Butler Yeats stayed up late one windy night writing a poem titled, "Prayer for My Daughter." In it he lamented that "arrogance and hatred are the wares/ peddled in the thoroughfares," and prayed that she would know something different, that someday her bridegroom would bring her to a house "where all's accustomed, ceremonious." In a word, a home suffused with grace.

I can't believe the thoroughfares are selling better wares a hundred years later.

But we are called to something different. In an age when manipulation is a science, and celebrityhood the unholy grail of the perpetual adolescent, we are called not to be ministered unto, but to minister, to serve.

Good service requires diligent preparation, and I hope you have worked hard. Good service, after all, is not just good intentions; we actually have to know what we're doing. We should all take to heart the first rule for physicians: First, do no harm.

You have heard maybe a couple of hundred times that our purpose here at Corban is to help prepare you to "make a difference in the world for Jesus Christ." Of course that includes planting churches, taking the gospel to the homeless and the runaway, working with orphans. We all know that.

But as we are called upon to oppose this present world, I'm urging you now, as you prepare to leave this university, to oppose this present world by living a life of dignity and grace. I hope that in an age of loud and corrupted airwaves and vicious electronic messages you will remember that Scripture commands, "Let your speech be always with grace, seasoned with salt."

In the graduate classroom, on the job, in our living room or kitchen—this is the kind of speech, the kind of demeanor, befitting those who represent the King of Kings, who derive our dignity and our strength from Him, to Whom be honor and glory, dominion and power, now and forever. Amen.

About the Author

Jim Hills is Professor of Humanities at Corban University in Salem, Oregon.

He began his teaching career in Southern California, but was drawn to the Pacific Northwest in 1973 by clean air, green mountains, and people who would rather fish than work overtime. He has taught at Corban ever since. He describes his work this way: "I spend my days dealing in love and hope."

In addition to his work at Corban University he has taught in Germany, Indonesia, and several area prisons.

Jim was born in Ithaca, New York. He met Bonnie, born on Long Island, at The Master's College in California. They married in 1965. They have four children, six grandchildren, and twin great grandchildren. Bonnie has photos at hand, and will send some if you ask.

Jim can be reached at jhills@corban.edu and (503) 375-8123.

Made in the USA
Lexington, KY
30 July 2015